Developing Programs for Faculty Evaluation

A Sourcebook for Higher Education

Richard I. Miller

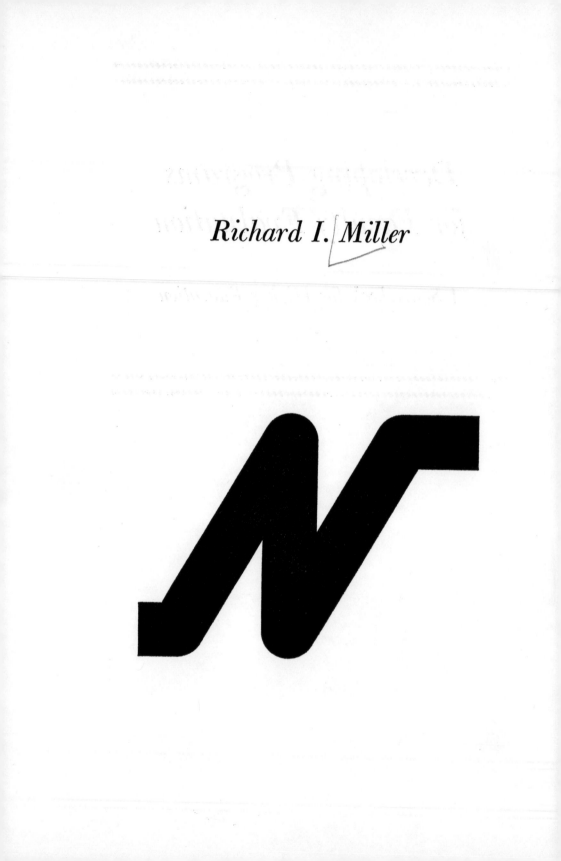

Developing Programs for Faculty Evaluation

Jossey-Bass Publishers

San Francisco • Washington • London • 1974

DEVELOPING PROGRAMS FOR FACULTY EVALUATION
A Sourcebook for Higher Education
by Richard I. Miller

Copyright © 1974 by: Jossey-Bass, Inc., Publishers
615 Montgomery Street
San Francisco, California 94111
&
Jossey-Bass Limited
3 Henrietta Street
London WC2E 8LU

Library of Congress Catalogue Card Number LC 73-12063

International Standard Book Number ISBN 0-87589-208-6

Manufactured in the United States of America

JACKET DESIGN BY WILLI BAUM

FIRST EDITION

Code 7402

The
Jossey-Bass Series
in Higher Education

Preface

In 1972 I wrote *Evaluating Faculty Performance* (Jossey-Bass), which sought to provide a comprehensive, sensitive, sensible, systematic, and manageable faculty evaluation program. Many professors and administrators found the ideas helpful, but problems in the creation of a total evaluation program obviously continued to plague many colleges and universities. The first book did consider strategies for instituting evaluative programs, but continued study and field activity brought home the need for increased emphasis on these strategies. Also, the need to provide additional resources for institutions developing their own programs became apparent. In faculty evaluation, as in many other areas, there is no single strategy, just multiple strategies. Each situation is unique, although there are elements common to almost all situations.

Most faculties have or are considering a system of evaluation, but some have already abandoned their evaluation programs. Why do these systems fail? We need professional autopsies, or analyses of crop failures, in education. Now we talk only about our expectations and successes, and even failures are twisted into successes. Most evaluation systems fail because of inadequate planning, poor programs (an obvious point that sometimes escapes those nearest to it), lack of involvement of key faculty, casual procedures for administering the evaluation instrument, inconsistent procedures for returning the instruments, slow processing time, confusion about who receives the results, application of results solely to promotion and tenure decisions, and excessive costs in time and money.

Developing Programs for Faculty Evaluation is designed to help professors and administrators avoid these problems. Its purpose is to serve as a resource in the development and maintenance of faculty evaluation systems rather than to present any one system. Those developing evaluation systems should find here useful references to the important studies on every phase of faculty evaluation, in addition to new ideas and strategies for implementation of programs. I also summarize a number of issues that are sensitive and timely.

This book is not a revision of *Evaluating Faculty Performance,* but a new volume. To provide aid to those setting up new programs, the Selected and Annotated Bibliography is extensive and is carefully indexed within the general indexes. Chapter Five, on administrative evaluation, is something of a first; more will be heard about this important area of evaluation in the future. And the case study of evaluation at Texas Christian University (Chapter Four) adds a fresh, on-campus dimension.

By providing both resources and strategies, *Developing Programs for Faculty Evaluation* should serve as a bridge between the researcher who does not have responsibility for program development and sometimes has very little interest in it and those who have program development responsibilities but are not technically competent in the field of faculty evaluation.

The support of my wife, Peggy, has been a source of encouragement in the countless hours spent in this enterprise, and our three daughters—Joan, Diane, and Janine—cooperated by holding the decibel level down to a tolerable level, at least most of the time!

Springfield, Illinois   Richard I. Miller
January 1974

Contents

Developing Programs
for Faculty Evaluation

A Sourcebook for Higher Education

Prologue

The current interest in faculty evaluation is unprecedented although by no means new. Interest existed in the twenties and thirties, and a noticeable spurt occurred in the late forties and early fifties, due largely to concern about the effects of increased enrollment and rapid expansion of faculty on the quality of classroom teaching. Some falling off took place in the sixties, probably due to the wealth of higher education while expansions in program and personnel sought to keep pace with growth in enrollment, and due to the large infusion of federal and state money. Student unrest in the midsixties and increasing fiscal constraints have further encouraged interest. The area continues to display the same vigor evident since about 1970, and continued growth in interest and programs of faculty evaluation can be expected. Administrative and institutional evaluations are likely to grow even faster because little has been done in either.

Faculty evaluation is linked to five critical issues in the management of higher education in the seventies, and closely linked to three of them. The latter are finance, governance, accountability, while flexibility and purpose are less closely related.

1

Finance

Sources of fiscal support for higher education will become more difficult in the decade ahead. To cite one example, Glenny at the 1973 annual meeting of the American Association of Colleges, quoted these figures: "In Connecticut in 1962, higher education institutions received $5\frac{1}{2}$ percent of the state's general revenue. By 1967 they received 12 percent. But the proportion has been diminishing since 1967, until in the past year it was $10\frac{1}{2}$ percent, $1\frac{1}{2}$ percent below its highest proportion in 1967. This decreasing proportion of state revenue occurred at the same time that a new medical school was brought up to a $16 million budget, new communities were developing, and aid to nonpublic institutions was increasing."

A reordering of fiscal priorities is taking place at the state level, and competition for the decreasing tax revenue is becoming more keen and more political. Transportation, security, correctional programs, welfare, health, elementary and secondary education, and other areas are competing vigorously with higher education for tax support. The federal level offers little encouragement in the way of additional revenue; indeed, its future is also bleak. Thus little new money can be expected for higher education in the next few years, at least. An occasional new program will surface only to be inundated by hundreds of eager research and development officers. About 1500 proposals were submitted by the April 15, 1973 deadline for the $10 million available from the FUND for the Improvement of Postsecondary Education—one of the very few new federal monies for innovation in postsecondary education in 1973.

As state funds become more scarce and state priorities place higher education in a more competitive position, with little new assistance expected from the federal government, what will happen to higher education in an economy where cost-of-living increases of 6 to 12 percent yearly are to be expected? Institutions of higher education will need to look inward toward "intensive growth," to use a phrase from Clark Kerr of the Carnegie Commission on Higher Education. Intensive growth includes better accountability and management procedures, such as various kinds of reallocation efforts, as well as creative ways of assisting university personnel in acquiring new skills. Scarcity of resources means fewer new positions and some existing ones phased out. Making these difficult decisions requires a broad and sound data base, and systematic faculty evaluation can serve as one data source.

Governance

The issues of institutional governance are coming into focus with the surge of collective bargaining, and have contributed to some professional reluctance to initiate or promote faculty evaluation even though the American Association of University Professors cosponsored a two-year study of the matter and developed some recommendations favoring it (Eble, 1970). Most collective bargaining agreements today pay little or no attention to faculty evaluation, assuming that better working conditions and better pay automatically result in better teaching—a questionable assumption. More creative models will probably include faculty evaluation because it is only reasonable to expect greater teaching effectiveness with increases in salaries and benefits. Also, provisions for merit increases may appear in collective bargaining agreements.

The faculty is demanding a greater voice in institutional governance, particularly in matters of promotion and tenure. These critical questions must be decided on the soundest data base possible, including evidence of teaching effectiveness from student ratings. Those who oppose use of student appraisals deny the single most important data basis for judging teaching effectiveness.

Accountability

Accountability means relating objectives sought to ends achieved. It can be measured in a number of ways, with the basic purpose of greater efficiency and effectiveness in human and material resource utilization to assist management in reaching specified objectives within the time planned. Precise accountability requires some systematic means of gathering, analyzing, and evaluating data, hence demands for improved methods of evaluating faculty performance can be expected—especially from state legislators.

Several quantitative outputs can be measured with reasonable accuracy, including instructional outcomes, degree and credit hour production, and costs of instruction as compared with costs of administration. Qualitative outputs, or benefits, of higher education are much more difficult to measure yet are closer to the purposes and goals of higher education. Enarson (1973) has written that the university is "a very special kind of place. It is more like the Metropolitan Opera than the Metropolitan Life Insurance Company."

Flexibility

The movement toward nontraditional delivery systems in postsecondary education was predicted in the 1962 Johnstone-Rivera study: "The most important conclusion to be derived from this study is that America is likely to experience an adult education explosion during the next few decades. . . . Just as in the fifties and sixties the regular school system had to tool up rapidly to accommodate the greatly increased numbers of young persons in the population, so too in the seventies and eighties adult education will be subject to greatly increased demands. . . ." (Johnstone-Rivera, 1965).

The nontraditional movement is basically personalized counseling plus individualized learning. Since it emphasizes the product (what is known) rather than the process (how it is acquired), there is less to evaluate. If a person passes a standardized examination for credit, about all he can evaluate is the quality of the examination, and the counseling process that led to his decision to sit for it.

Goals

"A society that does not believe in anything will never achieve excellence. What do Americans believe in? And how ardently do they believe? It is a timely question." These views from John Gardner's provocative treatise on *Excellence* are as timely as when he wrote them in 1961. The purposes of higher education have not changed basically since the days in ancient Greece when Isocrates set up a school emphasizing oratory and public affairs and Plato established his Academy to develop a person intellectually, physically, and emotionally equipped for leadership. Today we still have the same dichotomy between higher education with an occupation or career bias and higher education with an academic or intellectual bias or, expressed another way, between those who want to mesh education and the marketplace and those who prefer the intellectual atmosphere of the contained campus.

The trend toward career education has gained momentum in recent years, with impetus from the United States Office of Education and the community college movement. Evaluation becomes more difficult as programs are moved offcampus or as the marketplace comes onto the campus. This condition should challenge the creativity of evaluators rather than inhibit or cast aspersions on the desirability of this alternative.

The national scene has changed very considerably in the past decade, as pointed out by Cheit (1972):

> The problem of how to bring new faculty members in is becoming the problem of how to counsel old ones out. Those happy recruitment parties at the scholarly conventions are being replaced by dreary technical meetings on the actuarial foundations of early retirement.
>
> Those pioneering building problems—how to build space to house new faculty and new programs—have become the burdensome management problems of how to find budgeted activities to fill those buildings, and how to live with that most deceptive of euphemisms, deferred maintenance.
>
> Young faculty members were told their problem was to meet the established teaching, research, and service standards and their reward would be advancement to tenure. But now their problem is that we cannot always keep the promise, and our problem is that they are forming unions.
>
> Until recently, a persuasive argument for starting a new program was that "someone else is doing it." Today that fact is a respectable argument for *not* starting it.
>
> The problem of what to do with new money has become the problem of how to hang on to the old. Faculty positions that could not be filled at budgeted ranks, or filled at all, produced "budgetary savings," that most valuable of all academic resources, new money. New money was used to fund academic innovation and even whole departments, with pride. Now that enrollment trends are threatening to throw support

formulas into reverse, the remaining money is being used to fund management innovation and even whole management systems, with prayer.

In the office of student admissions, until recently the problem was how to buy. Today the problem is becoming how to sell. A recent advertisement in *The Chronicle of Higher Education* says "Learn How to Recruit More New Students For Your Institution." Admissions procedures that could humble the most confident applicant are fast on the way becoming candidates for human relations awards.

As for research grants, they have always been popular, but as John Gardner recalls from his service as Secretary of HEW during those golden years, academics were particular about the way they got the money. They insisted on the method he called the "leave it on the stump" approach. Now there is moss on the stump. The new way is the accountable way. At the annual meeting of the Association of Universities and Colleges of Canada this year the Director of Statistics of Canada set the tone by warning his colleagues that the "future will be an era of no growth," and the entire meeting was devoted to accountability in research funding.

Strategies for Developing a System

In mapping strategies for developing faculty evaluation, it is important to accept certain perspectives.

First, it should be recognized that there is a rich reservoir of research and study on the problems and techniques of faculty evaluation, going back well over 40 years. Programs were in operation shortly after World War II at Brooklyn College, Purdue University, the University of Washington, the University of Michigan, and others. Early works of Guthrie at the University of Washington and Remmers at Purdue University are still timely and useful. The tendency to rediscover the wheel may be diminished if these earlier reports are studied seriously. It is interesting to note that a substantial majority of the most eminent psychologists have dabbled in faculty evaluation at one time or another.

A second perspective concerns the quality of the research: it is far from uniform, and in some cases quite contradictory. Differences in size and type of institution may make a significant difference in the findings. Brooklyn College, for example, does differ substantially from West Virginia Wesleyan and therefore findings might well be different yet equally valid for the circumstances of each. Some research studies are simply better than others; and in still other cases the conclusions do not follow the data closely. Yet some valuable information can be achieved from the cluster approach. This technique does not evaluate the internal validity and quality of each study but accepts them—even though this assumption has admitted weaknesses. But the possibility of carefully analyzing each study is remote when several hundreds are involved, and the differences in the research design, size and nature of the institution, semantical ambiguities, and the era of the research can never be analyzed fully. So generalization from clusters of studies seems a logical way out of the thicket.

Another perspective is that the overriding purpose of faculty, administration, and institutional evaluation *must be to improve the instructional program*. This is not a play on words to con faculty into cooperation; indeed, if that is true the perceptive analyses of faculty members will discern the situation and make life difficult for those who say one thing and do another. Improvement in instruction means using the results to assist those who are faltering, to counsel those who are tired, and to encourage those who are uncertain. It may include attending refresher courses, working with acknowledged master teachers, undertaking special study programs, and so forth.

The results of faculty evaluation should be used to assist in decisions about promotion and tenure. The tenure decision is the most important one made about an individual faculty member, and on the basis of it the institution invests well over one-half million dollars in an individual, as well as setting long range developmental patterns. Current economic realities make these decisions even more important. A number of institutions have found departments tenured-in as a result of decisions made during the green days of higher education.

Personnel decisions need to be based on the broadest possible valid information. To do less denies the individual maximum opportunity to demonstrate his worth. If the data on faculty evaluation are valid and reliable—and they should not be used if they are not—then they can play an important role in personnel decisions. Of course, other inputs are needed also, including colleague opinion with all of its foibles and question marks (see Hildebrand's article on "How to Recommend Promotion for a Mediocre Teacher Without Actually Lying," 1971) and opinions of department heads and sometimes professors outside the university.

Use of data from faculty evaluation should follow carefully planned and understood procedures, to minimize the negative overtones that inevitably arise. It should be remembered that the weaknesses are offset by having a better data base for making the personnel decisions that must be made, and by spelling out the positive intent and operational aspects of the evaluation system.

And finally, in larger perspective: Evaluation is a means to larger ends; and colleges and universities must remain bastions of idealism and hope for a better tomorrow, and much in the spirit of John Masefield's poem, "There are few earthly things more beautiful than a university."

> It is a place where
> those who hate ignorance
> may strive to know . . .
>
> Where those who perceive truth
> may strive to make others see . . .
>
> Where seekers and learners alike,
> bonded together in the search for knowledge
> will honor thought in all its finer ways . . .
>
> Will welcome thinkers in distress or exile,
> will uphold ever the dignity of thought and
> learning, and exact standards in all these things.
>
> They give to the young in their impressionable
> years, the bond of lofty purpose shared,
> of a great corporate life
> whose links shall not be loosed until they die.
>
> They give to young people
> that close companionship
> for which youth longs . . .
>
> And that chance for endless discussion of themes
> which are endless—without which youth
> would seem a waste of time.

There are few earthly things
more splendid than a university . . .

In these days of broken frontiers
and collapsing values . . .

When dams are down
and the floods are making misery . . .

When every future looks somewhat grim . . .

And every ancient foothold . . .

Has become something of a quagmire.

Wherever a university stands it stands and
shines . . .

Wherever it exists, the free minds of men
urged on to full and fair inquiry,
may still bring wisdom into human affairs.[1]

A good beginning to developing an overall system of faculty
evaluation is to consider certain elements of the psychological process, such as the following:

Process is more important than product. This concept comes
hard to some academicians but administrators learn this generalization early as part of their survival kit. The stereotype of the salesman whose intolerable personality and behavior are tolerated because of his outstanding bottom–line performance exemplifies the
exception because studies on human relations and success indicate
that more positions are lost because of failures in human relations
than through technical or professional incompetence. A former university president, Frederic Ness (1972), explained the priorities this
way: "It takes less time to touch bases than to mend fences." But a
good thing can be carried too far, and excessive sensitivity can result in so much process that little is accomplished. Educators do not
err on this point, however, and generally zeal for an idea or program overshadows how to accomplish it. Hundreds of good ideas
float around and never go anywhere because no one has found a
way to mobilize the human and material resources necessary.

[1] Reprinted from *The Johns Hopkins Magazine,* February 1953.
Originally spoken at the University of Sheffield as part of Mr. Masefield's
toast of the Honorary Graduands on the occasion of the installation of the
chancellor in June 1946.

Evaluation systems are produced by people and therefore reflect their strengths and weaknesses, hopes, and fears. The following is an example of the process/product consideration: Upland State University has approximately 8000 undergraduate and graduate students. It is located in a semirural Midwestern environment that registered a ten percent population decline in the 1970 census. The decrease was reflected in student enrollment also. The university president, with more than gentle urging from the staff of the state board of higher education, decided to encourage the development of a comprehensive system of faculty evaluation. He also consulted his assistants and the academic vice-president, who was asked to discuss the matter with the college deans. The academic vice-president was a man of precision and action, wanting things to happen. He strongly fortified the president's interest, indeed, over-represented it so that some deans gained the impression that the president had made up his mind and wanted to move ahead as quickly as possible. The deans then presented the matter to their department chairmen, who in turn did likewise to faculty members. The presentations, taking the cue from the academic vice-president, were more presentations than discussion of exploratory sessions. Meanwhile, the academic vice-president, encouraged by the deans' response or lack of it, met with the executive committee of the faculty council. The five-member committee generally was sympathetic but one member insisted that the faculty be involved in developing the plan. This point was duly recognized by the academic vice-president but in his report to the president it received minimal attention. The president had established a pattern of setting up presidential committees with good results. He decided to follow the same procedure, and asked the academic vice-president to recommend seven members for the committee. The academic vice-president made a strategic error. Instead of approaching the executive committee on a parity basis for their nominations, he went first to the council of deans, then presented their nominations to the executive committee for consideration. The faculty group was asked to make nominations, too, but were reluctant to do so. The member who had expressed concern earlier was particularly vocal about what he considered an attempt to bypass the faculty. He had to work at developing this view because it was not altogether in keeping with the facts, but since he had privately opposed faculty evaluation this interpretation gave him a position that would be of concern to other faculty members also.

A year later, a well-designed and carefully prepared plan for faculty evaluation was rejected by the faculty, on grounds that much more time was needed for study and research. No action was taken to meet these objections. The real reason for disapproval was a year-long campaign by a relatively few faculty members (led by the executive committee member) to present the plan as an administratively contrived program to reduce faculty positions and use it for making decisions on promotion and tenure. This mini-case illustrates the extreme sensitivities that any plan for faculty evaluation can arouse. It also illustrates that process is more important than product.

Willingness to change is inversely proportional to proximity. It is easier to speak about needed reforms in Africa, in the university across town, or for that matter in another department, than to appraise the situation that touches one directly. Each of us has one voice saying, "Hold on to what is known and comfortable," and another saying, "There must be a better way." The physical location and nature of this continent and its history, and the background and traditions of a diverse immigrant population formed a natural home for pragmatism—a United States contribution to the field of philosophy. Yet the voice within us favoring tradition and non-change is ever present, as Francis Bacon noted in 1597: "It is true, that what is settled by custom, though it be not good, at least it is fit. And those things which have long gone together are as it were confederate within themselves; whereas new things piece not so well; but though they help by their utility, yet they trouble by their inconformity. Besides, they are like strangers, more admired and less favored."

Strategies for faculty evaluation need consider the Hegelian ambivalence that most individuals feel about change. Given this situation, how does change come about at all? The answer probably resides in a conglomerate of professionalism, self-interest, pride, and gentle pressures. Professional spurs such as self- and institutional improvement and prestige can be persuasive. "Every day in every way I am getting better and better" is a popularized version of the desire within us for human perfectibility—a drive deeply rooted in Judaic-Christian traditions. Self-interest recognizes the primacy of self in decisions, and it includes also self-satisfactions gained by those who develop, install, and operate a system of evaluation. They come to have a vested interest in seeing the system work and therefore they work hard for its success. Pride can serve as a constructive force for change when it motivates individuals to assist in keeping their institution abreast or in front of other institutions, or when it motivates professional betterment. Institutions, which are conglomerations of individuals, do not want to be viewed as behind the times. And finally, gentle pressures can be helpful, either from colleagues or the administration. The key word is *gentle*. The faculty is at the heart of the collegial enterprise and its members will not be pushed around by colleagues or administrators; yet sophisticated and gentle pressures can be applied with considerable leverage. But how about unsophisticated and direct pressure by the administration? In a few instances these procedures work although long-term viability of programs achieved by such means may be jeopardized by short-term gains. After all, faculty members watch deans and presidents come and go.

Expect opposition. Or in the vernacular of the backfield coach: Start leaning forward *before* you hit the line! A few professors on every faculty are unalterably opposed to faculty evaluation, believing with Gilbert Highet (1950) that "teaching is an art, not a science." One cannot deal with this opposition rationally because it is based essentially on feelings and intuition. Expect individuals with this view to resort to campus politics to persuade others of the futility and folly of all evaluative systems. This group, however, can assist proponents of evaluation by requiring rigorous thought on questions raised by them. Rather than spend time in a conversion effort, advocates of evaluation should work with those who favor the program or are openminded and neutral or at least rational in their opposition. Advocates need to be conversant with the research on evaluation and aware of sensitive and key issues. Also, they should be effective in the give-and-take of disputation.

Know your faculty. Or in terms of the ditty in *The Music Man,* you have got to know the territory! Centers or clusters of influence and power in every faculty must be considered carefully when planning for evaluation. Dressel (1961) identifies three contrasting patterns of thinking about education: The traditionalist is oriented to the past, the eclectic to the present, and the relativist to the future. Evans (1968) discusses the personality factors characteristic of the two prototypes, the innovator and laggard, the pro-instructional television (ITV) and the anti-ITV professor: "We found those who resisted ITV appeared to be more narrowly restricted in their interests within the university, that they carried larger teacher loads, that they tended to be more resistant to psychological testing, and that they tended to be a little more anxious in general. . . . We found significantly more resistance in certain disciplines, primarily in the humanities rather than in the technological fields. . . . The professor who favored ITV tended to extend his interest beyond the university, had broader interests, carried a smaller teaching load, and was often more productive in such nonteaching activities as writing and research." Based on a study of 1000 faculty members from a variety of institutions, Gaff and Wilson (1970) found *prochangers* were significantly more abundant in the lower ranks "and come from the humanities and social studies than from the natural sciences and applied fields." This finding differs from what Evans concluded about the attitudes of the various disciplines toward instructional television. Ladd and Lipset (1972), with a data base of over 60,000 professors, found that "all of the natural sciences . . . are significantly more conservative politically than the social sciences." And Centra (1972) found that students perceived natural science teachers less open to other viewpoints; humanities teachers were less likely to inform teachers of how they were to be evaluated. Centra's study focuses on student perceptions of professors while the other studies focus on how professors and administrators perceive professors. From these studies, one cannot discern a pattern in faculty attitudes on student evaluation. The sciences, it seems, tend to be more supportive and innovative about faculty evaluation than the humanities, but research is needed to test this hypothesis.

Keep strategy flexible and low-key. The strategy need not be shouted from the housetops nor locked in a vault. The committee or group developing the procedure needs to carefully tailor it to its own circumstances. The main thrust must be geared to the uniqueness of a particular campus. It is all right to discuss strategy in the abstract, for this may generate some creative ideas and approaches, but in

the concrete it needs to consider what should be done, how the objectives should be accomplished, who should be involved, and what
timetable should be used. Success is directly proportional to the
time and effort put into the process.

The following guidelines are elaborated on in *Evaluating
Faculty Performance* (pp. 17–18): support at the top, hard work,
trial runs, faculty resistance points, open hearings, and time for implementation. In his report on the Project to Improve College
Teaching, Eble (1970) suggests these steps for the establishment
and maintenance of a successful student evaluation: (1) Gaining
the cooperation of the faculty. (2) Defining purposes, objectives,
and uses. (3) Arriving at means and procedures. (4) Making crucial policy decisions. (5) Establishing an office for administering the
program. (6) Keeping the campus community informed. (7) Fi-
nancing a continuing program. (8) Maintaining student and faculty interest and involvement. (9) Conducting follow-up activities
and studies. (10) Relating evaluation to other efforts to recognize,
reward, and improve teaching.

2

Choosing Among Evaluative Criteria

E*valuating Faculty Performance* suggests that evaluation of overall faculty performance should consider nine categories: classroom teaching, advising, faculty service and relations, management (administration), performing and visual arts, professional services, publications, public service, and research. Obviously only a few criteria are appropriate in any particular case, but consideration of this broader range more than the traditional trilogy of teaching-research-service adds greater flexibility and realism to the process. Classroom teaching remains the dominant raison d'etre for colleges and universities and five aspects of it will be considered in this chapter, and the category of faculty service and relations will be discussed. But first, the teaching and/or research dilemma.

Teaching and/or Research

Much more heat than light has been generated on this issue over the years, and the matter is made more difficult in view of vast differences among the 2400 colleges and universities. The current presidents of Stanford University and the University of Chicago, for example, have stated institutional positions favoring research over teaching; and presidents of most small, and some not so small, institutions have stated a clear priority on teaching. So the first consideration in deciding how much weight to give teaching vs. research is the nature and purposes of the institution. The production of new knowledge by somebody somewhere, probably on campuses more than anywhere else, is essential for continued societal advancement. If some institutions want to give priority to theoretical and/or applied research, this position is valid and important to the larger state and national interest.

Most large universities, however, are more equivocal than Stanford or Chicago (both private institutions) on their research-teaching balance. The large land-grant universities are obliged to curry the favor of legislators, state board officials, and alumni by espousing the central importance of teaching. But one suspects that Hyman's observation (1973) is near the mark. He contends that "no single dogma is more central to the accepted philosophy of higher education than the notion that a university faculty member must be a scholar as well as a teacher. That concept shapes the university's structure; it controls the way we select our faculties, how we reward them, apportion their responsibilities, and what we expect of them." The large land-grant university, then, may have a double standard with respect to research-teaching. On the one hand it sincerely espouses and believes in the central importance of teaching, and the nature of its public image and support require it to do so. But professors who control the promotion and tenure committees feel that they must uphold the academic mystique of scholarship even though few do much research or scholarly study.

Smaller colleges, and especially private colleges, emphasize teaching; and since their circumstances seldom provide any viable alternative the issue is not teaching vs. research but how teachers can do sufficient research to keep abreast of techniques and discipline, or study research sufficiently to benefit from it. A famous French novelist, asked whether her experiences were the basis for her racy writing, replied: "One does not have to experience death to write about it!" But either some direct research or systematic study of the research of others seems essential if one is to stay abreast of any field of endeavor. It is difficult to see how a teacher who does neither can long remain an effective teacher. The obsolescence of knowledge in almost all fields is taking place at a rapid and accelerating pace. Yet the research by McDaniel and Feldhusen (1970), based on a sample of 76 professors and 4484 students at Purdue University, indicates that there is no relationship between writing books and teaching effectiveness. They found that the most effective instructors write no books and limit their roles as paper and article writers to second authorship; and there was no relationship between research activity, as indicated by grants, and instructional effectiveness. These findings, however, do not tell us whether the most effective instructors use research or how they keep up with developments in their field. Also, it would be interesting to do an age analysis of the McDaniel-Feldhusen data to see whether no major authorship over an extended period of time affects teaching effectiveness. The McDaniel and Feldhusen findings are contrary to those reached by Bresler (1968) in a study at Tufts University. He found that students rated as their best instructors those faculty members who had published articles and who had received or were receiving government support for research.

Colleges and universities with enrollments of 12,000 to 20,000 are caught in the teaching vs. research dilemma more than any others. Many are seeking to emulate the giant universities where research continues to have an established place, and many young professors in the middle-size institutions realize that entry into the larger, more prestigious universities requires an impressive record of publications and research.

Two generalizations flow from this discussion: Every college teacher needs to be an occasional, if modest, producer of research or creative work in his field; or at least a careful and systematic student of the research and creativity of others—and this involves more than a casual reading of scholarly journals. Research at the University of Southwestern Louisiana found that 10 percent of the faculty did 90 percent of the research, and about 30 percent of the faculty was engaged in research at any one time (Bourgeois, 1967). Assuming these figures vary from institution to institution, one can still conclude that research is a minor activity for most faculty members at moderate-size public institutions. When one takes the position that more research should be undertaken generally, this does not mean that "every kind of research effort," as mentioned by the American Academy of Arts and Sciences (1971), should be encouraged or undertaken. Some individuals say that teaching will suffer because so much time will go to research. This view is faulty from an institutional perspective because so little time is currently spent on research that a substantial increase would not need to detract from teaching, it could well come from nonteaching related activities that draw on many more hours than generally realized.

The teaching vs. research dilemma needs to be viewed in terms of the size and traditions of the institution. Institutional change does come about, but slowly—by accretion and attrition, according to JB Lon Hefferlin (1969). Individuals who have values and expectations that differ markedly from the institution should find another that is more compatible. A happy professional marriage is based on compatibility, similar lifestyles, and generally compatible expectations between the individual and the institution. The rub comes with younger faculty members who usually travel through several institutions to achieve their professional goals. These upwardly mobile young teachers may be out of phase with many colleagues because publications and research are very much part of their future employer's value pattern, if not their current one's. So once again the research vs. teaching dilemma comes in evidence. The solution finally rests with the individual professor, but he should make realistic choices in terms of his career interests, abilities, and those of institutions he serves and hopes to serve.

Classroom Teaching

Classroom teaching is the most central and important of the nine criteria that should be taken into account in a full-fledged evaluation program. Five types of assessment may be made of classroom teaching—student evaluations, classroom visitations, review of teaching materials and procedures, special incident reports, and self-evaluation. Problems in implementing classroom visitation, reviewing teaching materials and procedures, assessing special incidents, and making self-evaluations are covered here, while other issues relating to student evaluations occupy Chapter Three.

Visitation. Some dimensions of evaluation of overall professional performance should be the responsibility of colleagues, and the course content is particularly within the colleague sphere. (For colleague description forms developed by the Berkeley Center for Research and Development in Higher Education, see Forms 1 and 2.) Students are not in a strong position to judge the subject competence of the professor. Is his material current, is he sound in terms of his content mastery, does he bring various scholarly points of view to the students? Research on 1230 students at the University of Iowa (Stuit and Ebel, 1952) found that students felt significantly least competence in evaluating the instructor's "knowledge of his subject," when compared with several other items: clarity in explaining points, interest in class progress, friendliness and cooperativeness, enthusiasm for his subject, and fairness in examinations. Classroom visitation as well as the examination of teaching materials and procedures are colleague responsibility.

Classroom visitation has been a traditional aspect of teacher evaluation, going back to earlier and more relaxed days when the dean might drop in on a class, sit for a while, then leave. If nothing more was heard of the visit, the teacher could assume he passed inspection. Today we have moved toward the other end of the continuum and tend to establish too many procedures to insure fairness of the classroom observers and the process of observation when procedures cannot really do this. In one college of about 1000 students, the visiting team consists of the department head, a colleague of the teacher to be observed (presumably a friend who would be sympathetic!), and the academic dean. This procedure is an overkill in terms of professional time; and its structure, while bureaucratically sound, eventually may fall from its own weight.

The literature on classroom visitation is meager. Gage (1961) contends that teaching performance during observation may depend more on the teacher's nerve than anything else; Morton (1961) believes that the visitation should be done on more than one occasion and the evaluator should be supplied with course outline and briefed in advance on course content, purposes, and procedures. Estrin (1962) says that the department head should visit a class three times during the instructor's tenure year: the first as an orientation, the second to evaluate, and the third to summarize and confirm the reactions. And Hodgkinson (n.d.) in describing the classroom visitation procedure at Bard College, writes that "these evaluations are often longitudinal in nature in that they talk about the person's previous performance, where he now is, where he seems to go, and they usually mention some specific ways in which the person can be helped to get there. Thus they serve not only the purpose of being a decision-making device but also of providing a teacher with some specific ways in which he may improve, for use throughout the year."

Classroom visitation can provide helpful and useful data on classroom performance, and these guidelines are offered toward this end: The visiting team should be composed of two individuals: one in the teacher's discipline and one outside it, and respected, tenured faculty members. Members of the team should be selected by the dean, in consultation with the department chairman. Planning for the visitation should include the teacher who will be visited. The date of an initial visit should be set primarily by the teacher, and a synopsis or outline of the session should be distributed to the team at least one day before the visitation. A standardized appraisal form should be used. (*Evaluating Faculty Performance,* p. 33, contains a form for this purpose.) A form of some sort facilitates comparing data as well as provides a more systematic and objective consideration of teaching variables than a more informal approach might allow. A postsession with the teacher should take place no later than three days following the class visitation to discuss the observations and tentative conclusions of members of the observing team, provide the teacher with an opportunity to respond, and prepare a final report. The final report is filed with the dean, department head, and the teacher, who should have an opportunity to respond in writing if he wants to do so.

In addition to this approach, other possibilities should be considered. For example, Tyler (1958) suggests a list of conditions of learning for an observation checklist. He gives conditions for effective learning: student motivation; dissatisfaction with previous ways sets stage to try new ways; some guidance of the new behavior rather than by trial and error; appropriate materials; time for the activity and for subsequent practice; satisfaction from the desired behavior; a great deal of subsequent practice; high standards of per-

Form 1.
COLLEAGUE DESCRIPTION OF TEACHERS, SHORT FORM

INSTRUCTOR _____

DEPARTMENT _____

I. The following items reflect some of the ways teachers can be described. For the instructor named above, please circle the number which indicates the degree to which you feel each item is descriptive of him or her. In some cases, the statement may not apply to this individual. In these cases, check *Does not apply or don't know* for that item.

	Not at all *Descriptive*				*Very* *Descriptive*			*Doesn't apply* *or don't know*
	1	2	3	4	5	6	7	( )

1. Does original work that receives serious attention from others, corresponds with others about his work, expresses interest in colleagues' work, gives papers at conferences and keeps up with current developments

2. Is well read in and knowledgeable about his subject and related fields and is sought out by colleagues for advice on academic matters

3. Encourages students to talk with him, is involved in campus activities and has a congenial relationship with colleagues

4. Meets with students informally and is conscientious about appointments and office hours. Recognizes his students and encourages them to talk with him

5. Is interested in teaching, seeks advice and discusses teaching with colleagues. Is friendly toward and interested in the work of his colleagues

(Additional items may be presented by instructor and/or department)

FORM 1, 2.

II.

1. How does this instructor compare with other teachers at *this school?*

Among the very worst		About average				Among the very best
1	2	3	4	5	6	7

2. How does this instructor compare with other teachers in *this department?*

Among the very worst		About average				Among the very best
1	2	3	4	5	6	7

You are invited to comment further on the effectiveness of this instructor especially in areas not covered by the questions.

Source: **Developed by Robert C. Wilson and Evelyn R. Dienst, Center for Research and Development in Higher Education, University of California, Berkeley. Form CMF. Reproduced by permission of the authors.**

FORM 2.

COLLEAGUE DESCRIPTION OF TEACHERS, MEDIUM-LENGTH FORM

INSTRUCTOR ....

DEPARTMENT ....

I. The following items reflect some of the ways teachers can be described. For the instructor named above, please circle the number which indicates the degree to which you feel each item is descriptive of him or her. In some cases, the statement may not apply to this individual. In these cases, check *Does not apply or don't know* for that item.

	Not at all Descriptive		Very Descriptive			Doesn't apply or don't know
	1	2	3	4	5	( )

1. Does work that receives serious attention from others
2. Corresponds with others about his research
3. Does original and creative work
4. Expresses interest in the research of his colleagues
5. Gives many papers at conferences
6. Keeps current with developments in his field
7. Has done work to which I refer in teaching
8. Has talked with me about his research
9. Seems well read beyond the subject he teaches
10. Is sought by others for advice on research
11. Can suggest reading in any area of his general field
12. Knows about developments in fields other than his own
13. Is sought by colleagues for advice on academic matters
14. Encourages students to talk with him on matters of concern
15. Is involved in campus activities that affect students
16. Attends many lectures and other events on campus
17. Has a congenial relationship with colleagues

18. Meets with students informally out of class
19. Is conscientious about keeping appointments with students
20. Meets with students out of regular office hours
21. Encourages students to talk with him on matters of concern
22. Recognizes and greets students out of class
23. Seeks advice from others about the courses he teaches
24. Discusses teaching in general with colleagues
25. Is someone with whom I have discussed my teaching
26. Is interested in and informed about the work of colleagues
27. Expresses interest and concern about the quality of his teaching

(Additional items may be presented by instructor and/or department)

FORM 2, 3.

II. 1. How does this instructor compare with other teachers at *this school?*

	Among the very worst		*About average*			*Among the very best*
	1	2	3	4	5	6	7

2. How does this instructor compare with other teachers in *this department?*

	Among the very worst		*About average*			*Among the very best*
	1	2	3	4	5	6	7

You are invited to comment further on the effectiveness of this instructor especially in areas not covered by the questions

Source: Developed by Robert C. Wilson and Evelyn Dienst, Center for Research and Development in Higher Education, University of California, Berkeley. Form CSF. Reproduced by permission of the authors.

formance set by learner; and continued learning beyond the time when a teacher is available.

Care should be taken to avoid overbureaucratizing the process. Some procedures for classroom visitation are too complex and burdensome, with a system of checks and balances created to institute fairness. While the purpose is commendable, systems and procedures are only as effective as the goodwill and intentions of those operating them. It is better to have an acceptable system and then put maximum effort into selecting those visiting the classrooms and prompt and judicious use of the results. The perfection of the human aspects of the system will take time.

Materials and procedures. This criterion has been generally ignored and deserves greater attention. The judgment of this criterion must rest with colleagues, and it can be done any number of ways. One might be to have a colleague teaching the same subject and another teacher outside of the teacher's discipline go over course outlines and other distributed materials and make some judgments about their currency, academic soundness, relationship with the course objectives, and their level. Again, the results of the study should be shared with the teacher, and copies should go to the dean and department head. (See *Evaluating Faculty Performance,* p. 34, for a form that might be helpful.)

Assessing special incidents. This should be done in a systematic and judicial manner. Previously, special incidents were either filed mentally by the vice-president or dean, or else filed on a slip of paper and placed in the personnel folder. The administrators who continue in this archaic manner are asking for trouble. The courts have made clear that professors have the right to know the nature of the grievances against them, and to confront the evidence in keeping with the rights of any citizen under the Sixth Amendment. Accounts of special incidents that reflect adversely on the individual may be included in his personnel file but the contents and nature of the inclusion should be known to him, and the opportunity to respond in writing should be offered. Too often the absence of negative comments is taken as evidence of positive performance. Almost everyone with some experience in higher education knows at least one case in which promotion or tenure was denied capriciously, often on hearsay evidence or the opinions of a few persons. In the future, special incidents used as positive or negative evidence will have to stand the test of judicial procedures. This does place restrictions on the way personnel data are gathered and used but the loss is more than offset by the more professional approach that is judicially defensible.

Self-evaluations. These are not used to any noticeable extent in higher education, although most sensitive professors and administrators have learned and benefitted from self-evaluation. *Evaluating Faculty Performance* includes an appraisal form that can be used to assist in a more systematic approach to self-evaluation, and this form is comparable with forms for classroom visitation and student appraisal (see p. 37).

Research on self-evaluation is sketchy and not conclusive. Webb and Nolan (1955), reporting on the results of supervisor ratings, student ratings, and self-ratings at the Jacksonville Naval Air Technical Training School, found a high degree of correlation between student ratings and instructor self-ratings. However, the supervisor's ratings showed no correlation with any of the additional measures obtained: intelligence, level of schooling, teaching experience, or desire to teach. The more intelligent instructors, and those with more schooling, tended to be more self-critical. Those who expressed a greater desire to teach were rated superior teachers by their students. The discrepancy between student rating and instructor's ratings did not seem to be related to the judged proficiency of the teacher. And a study by Sorey (1968), using fifty college teachers, found that superior teachers showed more accuracy in their self-ratings and Guilford-Zimmerman scores than inferior teachers. But Centra (1972) in his comparative study of over 300 classes at five colleges found a modest relationship (.21) between students' ratings of instruction and the instructors' self-ratings and G-scores. The highest correlations occurred for the more factual items and the lowest on items eliciting opinions.

Self-evaluation should have a more prominent place in overall faculty and administrative evaluation. Dressel (1970) states that self-evaluation is essential to improvement, and any kind of evaluation will be resented and rejected until an individual confronts his professional weaknesses. Eble (1970) writes that we have probably passed the peak for institutional self-studies, and with it the peak of interest in faculty self-evaluation as a means of improving instruction. Perhaps Eble's view, formulated in 1969 or 1970, is a reflection of that period but the current fiscal austerity in higher education that is prompting the ascendancy of resource allocation and program priorities have made institutional self-study more prominent than anytime since the late fifties and early sixties; and the introspective thrust in human relations and psychology has given renewed impetus to self-evaluation.

Self-evaluation can take place in several ways. One that has proven effective relates to student appraisal forms. The form is given students during the first two weeks of the term and results are for the instructors' eyes only. This early appraisal can be helpful in spotting weaknesses or areas that need greater attention. And a second student rating near the end of the term can be compared with the earlier one for improvement as well as for appraisal of overall teaching effectiveness. A second kind of evaluation may consist of spending part of one class period in a face-to-face class evaluation. This procedure has some drawbacks and it would not fit some instructors' personalities, but it has been used effectively. And finally, self-evaluation needs administrative support and encouragement. Promotion and tenure definitely should include qualitative self-evaluation along with the usual laundry-list or brag-sheet type of data. Questions might include: What are my teaching accomplishments during the academic year? What are my greatest academic strengths? What are my greatest academic weaknesses? What aspects of my overall college contribution should be considered? Clearly, self-evaluation, in addition to being the mark of successful performance in any endeavor, has a distinct place in overall faculty and administrative evaluation.

In conclusion, the problems and dilemmas of choosing among the nine criteria is evident to everyone in academe; but again, it should emphasize the value of optimum flexibility and individualization in using the criteria. And joint planning between the teacher and the department head is critical to success. A college or department that weighs everyone's contributions according to some predetermined formula (for example, everyone must teach, advise, and do service) is taking an unimaginative and bland position—one that is miles away from the excitement and creativity that needs always to surround the academic enterprise. The individualized approach is more difficult to manage but it represents a sounder professional approach, and its messiness will be more than balanced by gains in faculty morale.

3

Using Student
Evaluations

If one is forced to choose the most significant component of evaluating classroom teaching, it would be student evaluation, although the use of several components are preferable to any single one. The evidence clearly indicates that students can evaluate teaching fairly and perceptively. Burton (1956) points out that students are in a better position than colleagues or administrators to judge the quality of instruction they are receiving, and the American Academy of Arts and Sciences (1971) states that "student opinion . . . is crucial" in identifying and rewarding successful teachers. And some time earlier, Aristotle, in *Politics,* pointed out that we receive a better notion of the merits of the dinner from the guests than from the cook! Bryant (1967), however, considers students too immature to evaluate effective teaching, and Fahey (1970) while favoring student-rating scales raises several cautions. Research by Rodin and Rodin (1972) based on results from 293 students in a large undergraduate calculus course indicates that students are less than perfect judges of teaching effectiveness if the latter is measured by how much they have learned; in fact, they conclude that good teaching is not validly measured by student evaluations in their current form. (For a critique of the Rodin article, see Centra's letter in the bibliography.) The substantial majority of those who have written on the matter, however, conclude that students can evaluate fairly and perceptively.

Classroom Effectiveness

What characteristics or qualities of college teaching do students relate to classroom effectiveness? French (1957) found that the ten items which contributed most to overall judgment at the University of Washington were: interprets abstract ideas and theories clearly, interests student in the subject, increases skills in thinking, broadens interests, stresses important material, makes good use of examples and illustrations, motivates to do best work, inspires class confidence in teacher's knowledge of the subject, provides new viewpoints or appreciations, and explains clearly. French pointed out that five of these were among the top ten items found by Guthrie (1954) in his studies more than a generation earlier. More recently, Crawford and Bradshaw (1968) asked students to describe their most effective college teacher, and the four most frequently mentioned characteristics were: thorough knowledge of subject matter; well-planned and organized lectures; enthusiastic, energetic, lively interest in teaching; and student-oriented, friendly, willing to help students. Although phrased somewhat differently, these characteristics resemble the ones appearing in French's list. (For characteristics of good teaching identified by others, see Table 1.) Also, the qualities identified by students correlate well with those given by professors. Gaff and Wilson (1971), Hildebrand (1971), and Lovell and Haner (1955) found good agreement between student and faculty ratings although Guthrie (1949) did not.

Questions of reliability and validity of student ratings inevitably arise. The evidence on the reliability is clear and consistent. Good reliability can be expected. The picture of reliability over time is also consistent in that the ratings of alumni correlate well with earlier ratings as students or with students currently studying with the same professors (Centra, 1973; Drucker and Remmers, 1950; Heilman, 1936; and Perry, 1969). We can count on the reliability of student-rating scales.

Table 1. CHARACTERISTICS

Bousfield[1]	Clinton[2]	Deshpande, et al[3]	French[4]
Fairness	Knowledge of subject matter	Motivation	Interprets ideas clearly
Mastery of subject	Pleasing personality	Rapport	Develops student interest
Interesting presentation of material	Neatness in appearance and work	Structure	Develops skills of thinking
Well-organized material	Fairness	Clarity	Broadens interests
Clearness of exposition	Kind and sympathetic	Content mastery	Stresses important materials
Interest in students	Keen sense of humor	Overload (too much work)	Good pedagogical methods
Helpfulness	Interest in profession	Evaluation procedure	Motivates to do best work
Ability to direct discussion	Interesting presentation	Use of teaching aids	Knowledge of subject
Sincerity	Alertness and broadmindedness	Instructional skills	Conveys new viewpoints
Keenness of intellect	Knowledge of methods	Teaching styles	Clear explanations
1. Listed in order of importance, by 61 undergraduates at University of Connecticut.	2. Listed in order of importance, by 177 junior-year students at Oregon State University.	3. Listed in order of importance, by 674 undergraduates who rated 32 engineering teachers.	4. Listed in order importance, by by undergraduates at the University of Washington.

We have less evidence on validity. Does the scale measure what it purports to measure, that is, good teaching? Or how do we know that those professors who receive good scores on student ratings are indeed good teachers? Some studies are available (Creager, 1950; Hildebrand, 1971; McKeachie, 1971) which indicate that student-rating scales can be considered valid procedures for assessing the quality of good teaching.

OF GOOD TEACHING

Gadzella[5]	Perry[6]	Pogue[7]	Hildebrand[8]
Knowledge of subject	Well-prepared for class	Knowledge of subject	Dynamic and energetic person
Interest in subject	Sincere interest in subject	Fair evaluator	Explains clearly
Flexibility	Knowledge of subject	Explains clearly	Interesting presentation
Well-prepared	Effective teaching methods		Enjoys teaching
Uses appropriate vocabulary	Tests for understanding		Interest in students
	Fair in evaluation		Friendly toward students
	Effective communication		Encourages class discussion
	Encourages independent thought		Discusses other points of view
	Course organized logically		
	Motivates students		
5. Listed in order of importance, by 443 undergraduates at Western Washington State College.	6. Listed in order of importance, by 1493 students, faculty, alumni at University of Toledo.	7. Listed in order of importance, by 307 students at Philander Smith College.	8. Listed in order of importance, by 338 undergraduate and graduate students at University of California, Davis.

Some opponents of student-rating forms contend that the teaching-learning process is too complex to be captured by any set of words, and some nonverbal dimensions defy words. One can agree—to a point. The teaching-learning process is difficult to capture with words but so are love, hate, empathy, confidence, and a myriad of less tangible complex emotions and activities. Yet these feelings are more successfully subject to clinical treatment than to mystical aspersions. Also, we know more about the teaching-learn-ing process than some critics of evaluation would lead us to believe, probably because this area of research and study is not familiar to them. The argument of complexity, therefore, cannot be considered adequate justification for *not* using student-rating forms, especially because evaluation in some form by somebody does take place.

The argument of student immaturity is less frequently ar-ticulated, but it is significant in the minds of many who oppose student-rating scales. The immaturity argument is related to a pa-triarchal concept of teacher-learner and a carryover from the more formal relationships of an earlier era, which indicates the age of many individuals who take this position. The position is faulty on two counts: First, it does not consider the students, themselves. Kenneth Keniston has written that "students are pushed into early maturity both intellectually and emotionally. One study suggests that the average student today stands one standard deviation above the average student a generation ago; that is, in testing performance and reasoning ability. In his parent's generation he would have been in the top 15 percent of his class. We also know that the age of puberty is decreasing at the rate of well over one-fifth of a year every decade so puberty comes more than two years earlier than it did in 1900. We know also that, roughly speaking, the amount of education students get is increasing by one year per decade. Com-pared to 40 years ago, students receive at least five years more edu-cation." (Mead Educational Services, 1970). Students today are simply more mature and have had considerable experience in evalu-ating and in being evaluated. And the immaturity position is based on a concept of teaching as telling or the receptacle theory of learn-ing. Teaching is telling, but it is much more: It is provoking, chal-lenging, puzzling, experimenting, weighing, choosing, reconsidering —it is a many-splendored thing that brings into play a broad spec-trum of teacher-learner interactions far beyond the traditional teaching-as-telling approach.

Choosing forms. Choosing instruments for student appraisal of teaching, has received little attention in the literature, yet the process commands considerable time of almost every committee established to study and implement faculty evaluation. Committees usually seek to invent their own rating scales—or rediscover the wheel. If this exercise increases acceptability of what is developed, then the hundreds or thousands of hours spent in developing an instrument may be justified, but normally the selection of an evaluative instrument is one of the *least* important factors in the overall evaluation procedure. It is better to analyze several established rating scales that have a research base. The Educational Testing Service (ETS) has developed a rating scale, for a price. (See Form 3.) The ETS instrument (1971) is based on the Michigan State University scale (Form 4; Warrington, 1972), which is also the basis for the one developed and described in *Evaluating Faculty Performance*. Short and long forms developed by the Berkeley Center for Research and Development on Higher Education (Wilson and Dienst, 1971) may be studied (see Forms 5 and 6), and the Purdue rating scale (Form 7; Remmers and Weisbrodt, 1965) has been used for well over 30 years and can be processed by Purdue, for a price. The Texas Christian University instrument and the research on it are included in this book as an original case study. Also included are the instruments used at Princeton University (see Form 8) and the University of Washington. (See Form 9.)

The Illinois Course Evaluation Questionnaire (Form 10; Spencer and Aleamoni, 1970) has been normed across several institutions. These rating scales by no means exhaust the list, but in any case, the cardinal rule is *adapt*—not adopt—an instrument. Adaptations are facilitated because most scales have a number of blank spaces where additional questions may be included.

The adaptive process might begin with some criteria by which the various instruments can be judged. Halstead (1970) has written that an adequate rating scale should contain four components: an underlying theory of instruction or a model of the instructional process, a translation of the theory or model into one or more operational definitions, development of a rating scale consistent with operational definitions, and assurance that student raters understand the criteria. Or the adaptive process might begin with a definition of good teaching, then various rating scales could be scrutinized to see how items related to various dimensions of this definition. In practice, however, most rating scales developed by individual institutions begin with a dragnet or popularity approach, or with the consequences rather than with the objectives. They usually begin with a request from the faculty for possible items, then computerize and rank-order the items. Interestingly, lists prepared this way do not differ appreciably from more conceptually derived statements. And they may be much more politically viable, since large numbers of faculty members have been involved in a matter close to them.

Two additional factors—the ease of use and the cost of administration—are important when choosing an instrument. A one-page instrument is preferable to a longer version, and comparisons of the long and short versions of the Berkeley instrument studied by the University of California at Davis indicates that the short form does almost everything achieved by the longer one.

The cost is a matter for each institution to decide, but it can be a considerable deterrent. Smaller campuses may not need to computerize the operation but machine assistance is necessary on middle-size and large campuses. Several variations might be considered if cost is a factor. For example, the rating scale might be given to students once each academic year; it may be given to only one of four classes; or it may be administered to every other student on a random basis.

Procedures for administering. The subtle but important factors related to how the rating system is administered often are given inadequate attention. For example, Kirchner (1969) found that student ratings were significantly higher when the instructor being rated was in the room than when he was absent. And Colliver (1972) found that students who do not sign the evaluation forms give significantly lower evaluations than those who do. Whether the instructor is in or out of the room when the students are completing the rating scales is not important, but consistency in how the ratings are administered is, if comparable results are expected or desired. And even if no comparison is sought, the teacher is unknowingly penalized by leaving the room when students are completing the form.

One procedure used at a number of institutions seems fairly simple and effective: All ratings forms are distributed and completed within a one-week period. The teacher distributes the forms and reads a standard statement to the class, outlining the process. The teacher leaves the room and an assistant from the class is appointed to gather the completed forms. The assistant then places all forms in a large brown envelope, seals the envelope before the class,

Text continued on Page 59

FORM 3.
STUDENT INSTRUCTIONAL REPORT

This questionnaire gives you an opportunity to express anonymously your views of this course and the way it has been taught.

> NA — *Not Applicable or don't know.* The statement does not apply to this course or instructor, or you simply are not able to give a knowledgeable response.

> SA — *Strongly Agree.* You strongly agree with the statement as it applies to this course or instructor.

> A — *Agree.* You agree more than you disagree with the statement as it applies to this course or instructor.

> D — *Disagree.* You disagree more than you agree with the statement as it applies to this course or instructor.

> SD — *Strongly Disagree.* You strongly disagree with the statement as it applies to this course or instructor.

SECTION I—Items 1-20:

1. The instructor's objectives for the course have been made clear

2. There was considerable agreement between the announced objectives of the course and what was actually taught........

3. The instructor used class time well......................

4. The instructor was readily available for consultation with students

5. The instructor seemed to know when students didn't understand the material...

6. Lectures were too repetitive of what was in the textbook(s)....

7. The instructor encouraged students to think for themselves....

8. The instructor seemed genuinely concerned with students' progress and was actively helpful..........................

9. The instructor made helpful comments on papers or exams....

10. The instructor raised challenging questions or problems for discussion ....

11. In this class I felt free to ask questions or express my opinions..

12. The instructor was well-prepared for each class.............

13. The instructor told students how they would be evaluated in the course ....

14. The instructor summarized or emphasized major points in lectures or discussions.....................................

15. My interest in the subject area has been stimulated by this course

16. The scope of the course has been too limited; not enough material has been covered................................... ....

17. Examinations reflected the important aspects of the course..... ....

18. I have been putting a good deal of effort into this course...... ....

19. The instructor was open to other viewpoints................. ....

20. In my opinion, the instructor has accomplished (is accomplishing) his objectives for the course........................ ....

SECTION II—Items 21-31:

21. For my preparation and ability, the level of difficulty of this course was:
    Very elementary ....
    Somewhat elementary ....
    About right ....
    Somewhat difficult ....
    Very difficult ....

22. The work load for this course in relation to other courses of equal credit was:
    Much lighter ....
    Lighter ....
    About the same ....
    Heavier ....
    Much heavier ....

23. For me, the pace at which the instructor covered the material during the term was:
    Very slow ....
    Somewhat slow ....
    Just about right ....
    Somewhat fast ....
    Very fast ....

24. To what extent did the instructor use examples or illustrations to help clarify the material?
    Frequently ....
    Occasionally ....
    Seldom ....
    Never ....

25. Was class size satisfactory for the method of conducting the class?
    Yes, most of the time ....

No, class was too large ....

No, class was too small ....

It didn't make any difference one way or the other ....

26. Which *one* of the following best describes this course for you?

Major requirement or elective within major field ....

Minor requirement or required elective outside major field.. ....

College requirement but not part of my major or minor field ....

Elective not required in any way ....

Other ....

27. Which *one* of the following was your most important reason for selecting this course?

Friend(s) recommended it ....

Faculty advisor's recommendation ....

Teacher's excellent reputation ....

Thought I could make a good grade ....

Could use pass/no credit option ....

It was required ....

Subject was of interest ....

Other ....

28. What grade do you expect to receive in this course?

A	....	....	Fail	....	....
B	....	....	Pass	....	....
C	....	....	No credit	....	....
D	....	....	Other	....	....

29. What is your approximate cumulative grade-point average?

3.50-4.00	....	....	1.00-1.49	....	....
3.00-3.49	....	....	Less than 1.00	......	....
2.50-2.99	....	....	None yet—freshman		
2.00-2.49	....	....	or transfer	....	....
1.50-1.99	....	....			

30. What is your class level?

Freshman	....	....	Senior	....	....
Sophomore	....	....	Graduate	....	....
Junior	....	....	Other	....	....

31. Sex

| Female | .... | .... | Male | .... | .... |

SECTION III—Items 32-39:

Legend 32-38: (1) Not applicable, don't know, or there were none. (2) Excellent. (3) Good. (4) Satisfactory. (5) Fair. (6) Poor.

	(1)	(2)	(3)	(4)	(5)	(6)
32. Overall, I would rate the textbook(s)	......	......	......	......	......	......
33. Overall, I would rate the supplementary readings	......	......	......	......	......	......
34. Overall, I would rate the quality of the exams.	......	......	......	......	......	......
35. I would rate the general quality of the lectures	......	......	......	......	......	......
36. I would rate the overall value of class discussions	......	......	......	......	......	......
37. Overall, I would rate the laboratories	......	......	......	......	......	......
38. I would rate the overall value of this course to me as	......	......	......	......	......	......

39. Compared to other instructors you have had (secondary school and college), how effective has the instructor been is this course?

    One of the most effective (among the top 10%) ....

    More effective that most (among the top 30%) ....

    About average... ....

    Not as effeective as most (in the lowest 30%) ....

    One of the least effective (in the lowest 10%) ....

SECTION IV—Items 40-49:

If the instructor provided supplementary questions and response options, use this section for responding.

40.	42.	44.	46.	48. ......
41.	43.	45.	47.	49. ......

If you would like to make additional comments about the course or instruction, use a separate sheet of paper. You might elaborate on the particular aspects you liked most as well as those you liked least. Also, how can the course or the way it was taught be improved? *Please Give these Comments to the Instructor.*

For further information write: Student Instructional Report, Educational Testing Service, Princeton, New Jersey 08540.

FORM 4.

STUDENT INSTRUCTIONAL RATING SYSTEM FORM

SA — if you *strongly agree* with the statement
A — if you *agree* with the statement
N — if you *neither* agree or disagree
D — if you *disagree* with the statement
SD — if you *strongly disagree* with the statement

Please omit any of the items which do not pertain to the course that you are rating. For example, if you have had no homework assignments in this course omit (leave blank) those items pertaining to home work.

1. The instructor was enthusiastic when presenting course material. ....
2. The instructor seemed to be interested in teaching........... ....
3. The instructor's use of examples or personal experiences helped to get points across in class............................ ....
4. The instructor seemed to be concerned with whether the students learned the material............................ ....
5. You were interested in learning the course material........... ....
6. You were generally attentive in class........................ ....
7. You felt that this course challenged you intellectually......... ....
8. You have become more competent in this area due to this course. ....
9. The instructor encouraged students to express opinions........ ....
10. The instructor appeared receptive to new ideas and others' viewpoints. ....
11. The student had an opportunity to ask questions............ ....
12. The instructor generally stimulated class discussion.......... ....
13. The instructor attempted to cover too much material........ ....
14. The instructor generally presented the material too rapidly..... ....
15. The homework assignments were too time consuming relative to their contribution to your understanding of the course material. ....
16. You generally found the coverage of topics in the assigned readings too difficult................................ ....
17. The instructor appeared to relate the course concepts in a systematic manner............................ ....
18. The course was well organized............................ ....
19. The instructor's class presentations made for easy note taking... ....
20. The direction of the course was adequately outlined.......... ....
21. You generally enjoyed going to class........................ ....

22. ⎫
23. ⎬ (Instructor may insert three (3) items.)
24. ⎭

STUDENT BACKGROUND: Select the most appropriate alternative.

25. Was this course required in your degree program?...........

26. Was this course recommended to you by another student?.....

27. What is your overall GPA? (a) 1.9 or less (b) 2.0-2.2 (c) 2.3-
   2.7 (d) 2.8-3.3 (e) 3.4-4.0............................

28. How many other courses have you had in this department? (a)
   none (b) 1-2 (c) 3-4 (d) 5-6 (e) 7 or more..............

29. ⎫
30. ⎬ (Instructor may insert two (2) items.)

Do not write below this line unless this course has laboratory or recitation sections

LABORATORY OR RECITATION: (fill in your recitation or lab number at the bottom)

31. The laboratory or recitation instructor clarified lecture material.

32. The laboratory or recitation instructor adequately prepared you
   for the material covered in his section.....................

33. You generally found the laboratories or recitations interesting...

34. ⎫
35. ⎬ (Instructor may insert two (2) items.)

WRITTEN COMMENTS: One way in which an instructor can improve his class is through thoughtful student reactions. The instructor hopes to use your responses for self-examination and self-improvement. If you have any comments to make concerning the instructor or the course, please write them below.

NOTE: The Student Instructional Rating System (SIRS) consists of the form (above), the report (computer printout), the manual (for users), the technical bulletin (describes SIRS development), Testing and Evaluation Bulletin 9 (a brief description of SIRS), and a series of SIRS Technical Reports: 1—Analysis of SIRS Responses for Winter Term 1970, 2—Stability of SIRS Factor Structure, 3—Using the SIRS in the Decision-making Process, and 4—SIRS Responses and Student Characteristics. SIRS materials are not copyrighted. For further information, write the Office of Evaluation Services, Michigan State University, East Lansing, Michigan 48824.

FORM 5.

STUDENT DESCRIPTION OF TEACHERS, SHORT FORM

INSTRUCTOR ....

DEPARTMENT ....

COURSE NUMBER OR TITLE ....

I. The following items reflect some of the ways teachers can be described in and out of the classroom. For the instructor named above, please circle the number which indicates the degree to which you feel each item is descriptive of him or her. In some cases, the statement may not apply to this individual. In these cases, check *Does not apply or don't know* for that item.

	Not at all Descriptive				Very Descriptive			Doesn't apply or don't know
	1	2	3	4	5	6	7	( )

1. Has command of the subject, presents material in an analytic way, contrasts various points of view, discusses current developments, and relates topics to other areas of knowledge.

2. Makes himself clear, states objectives, summarizes major points, presents material in an organized manner, and provides emphasis.

3. Is sensitive to the response of the class, encourages student participation, and welcomes questions and discussion.

4. Is available to and friendly towards students, is interested in students as individuals, is himself respected as a person, and is valued for advice not directly related to the course.

5. Enjoys teaching, is enthusiastic about his subject, makes the course exciting, and has self-confidence.

(Additional items may be presented by instructor and/or department)

FORM 5 (*cont.*)

II.

1. How does the instructor of this course compare with other teachers you have had at *this school?*

	Among the very worst		*About average*			*Among the very best*
	1	2	3	4	5	6	7

2. How does the instructor of this course compare with other teachers you have had in *this department?*

	Among the very worst		*About average*			*Among the very best*
	1	2	3	4	5	6	7

You are invited to comment further on the course and/or effectiveness of this instructor especially in areas not covered by the questions.

Source: Developed by Robert C. Wilson and Evelyn R. Dienst, Center for Research and Development in Higher Education, University of California, Berkeley. Form SSF-3. Reproduced by permission of the authors.

STUDENT DESCRIPTION OF TEACHERS, LONG FORM

INSTRUCTOR ....

DEPARTMENT ....

COURSE NUMBER OR TITLE ....

I. The following items reflect some of the ways teachers can be described in and out of the classroom. For the instructor named above, please circle the number which indicates the degree to which you feel each item is descriptive of him or her. In some cases, the statement may not apply to this individual. In these cases, check *Does not apply or don't know* for that item.

	Not at all Descriptive		Very Descriptive			Doesn't apply or don't know
	1	2	3	4	5	( )

1. Discusses points of view other than his own

2. Contrasts implications of various theories

3. Discusses recent developments in the field

4. Presents origins of ideas and concepts

5. Gives references for more interesting and involved points

6. Presents facts and concepts from related fields

7. Emphasizes conceptual understanding

8. Explains clearly

9. Is well prepared

10. Gives lectures that are easy to outline

11. Is careful and precise in answering questions

12. Summarizes major points

13. States objectives for each class session

14. Identifies what he considers important
15. Encourages class discussion
16. Invites students to share their knowledge and experiences
17. Clarifies thinking by identifying reasons for questions
18. Invites criticism of his own ideas
19. Knows if the class is understanding him or not
20. Knows when students are bored or confused
21. Has interest in and concern for the quality of his teaching
22. Has students apply concepts to demonstrate understanding
23. Has a genuine interest in students
24. Is friendly toward students
25. Relates to students as individuals
26. Recognizes and greets students out of class
27. Is accessible to students out of class
28. Is valued for advice not directly related to the course
29. Respects students as persons
30. Is a dynamic and energetic person
31. Has an interesting style of presentation
32. Seems to enjoy teaching
33. Is enthusiastic about his subject
34. Seems to have self-confidence
35. Varies the speed and tone of his voice
36. Has a sense of humor

(*Additional items may be presented by instructor and/or department*)

FORM 6 (cont.)

II.

1. How does the instructor of this course compare with other teachers you have had at *this school?*

Among the *very worst*		*About* *average*		*Among the* *very best*		
1	2	3	4	5	6	7

2. How does the instructor of this course compare with other teachers you have had in *this department?*

Among the *very worst*		*About* *average*		*Among the* *very best*		
1	2	3	4	5	6	7

You are invited to comment further on the course and/or effectiveness of this instructor especially in areas not covered by the questions.

Source: Developed by Robert C. Wilson and Evelyn R. Dienst, Center for Research and Development in Higher Education, University of California, Berkeley. Form SMF. Reproduced by permission of the authors.

THE PURDUE RATING SCALE FOR INSTRUCTION

Note to Instructors: To keep conditions as nearly uniform as possible, it is imperative that no instructions be given to the students. The rating scale should be passed out without comment at the beginning of the period.

Note to Students: Following is a list of qualities that, taken together, tend to make any instructor the sort of instructor that he is. Of course, no one is ideal in all of these qualities, but some approach this ideal to a much greater extent than do others. To provide information which may lead to the improvement of instruction, you are asked to rate your instructor on the indicated qualities by darkening one of the spaces on the line at the point which most nearly describes him with reference to the quality you are considering. For example, under Interest in Subject if you think your instructor is not as enthusiastic about his subject as he should be, but is usually more than mildly interested, darken the space marked 0D on the answer card.

	0A	0B	0C	0D	0E	0F	0G	0H	0I	0J
0. Interest in Subject		Always appears full of his subject.			Seems mildly interested.				Subject seems irksome to him.	

This rating is to be entirely impersonal. Do not sign your name or make any other mark on the paper which could serve to identify the rater.

	1A	1B	1C	1D	1E	1F	1G	1H	1I	1J
1. Interest in Subject		Always appears full of his subject.			Seems mildly interested.				Subject seems irksome to him.	

	2A	2B	2C	2D	2E	2F	2G	2H	2I	2J
2. Sympathetic Attitude toward Students		Always courteous and considerate.			Tries to be considerate but finds it difficult at times.				Entirely unsympathetic and inconsiderate.	

	3A	3B	3C	3D	3E	3F	3G	3H	3I	3J
3. Fairness in Grading		Absolutely fair and impartial to all.			Shows occasional favoritism.				Constantly shows partiality.	

	A	B	C	D	E	F	G	H	I	J
4. Liberal and Progressive Attitude			Welcomes differences in viewpoint.			Biased on some things but usually tolerant.			Entirely intolerant, allows no contradiction.	
5. Presentation of Subject Matter			Clear, definite and forceful.			Sometimes mechanical and monotonous.			Indefinite, involved, and monotonous.	
6. Sense of Proportion and Humor			Always keeps proper balance; not over-critical or over-sensitive.			Fairly well balanced.			Over-serious; no sense of relative values.	
7. Self-reliance and Confidence			Always sure of himself; meets difficulties with poise.			Fairly self-confident; occasionally disconcerted.			Hesitant, timid, uncertain.	
8. Personal Peculiarities			Wholly free from annoying mannerisms.			Moderately free from objectionable peculiarities.			Constantly exhibits irritating mannerisms.	
9. Personal Appearance			Always well groomed; clothes neat and clean.			Usually somewhat untidy; gives little attention to appearance.			Slovenly; clothes untidy and ill-kept.	
10. Stimulating Intellectual Curiosity			Inspires students to independent effort; creates desire for investigation.			Occasionally inspiring; creates mild interest.			Destroys interest in subject; makes work repulsive.	

Source: Copyright 1950 The Purdue Research Foundation, Purdue University. Developed by H. H. Remmers and D. N. Elliott.

COURSE EVALUATION

NOTE: The course evaluation questionnaire (which is copyrighted by Princeton University) is in the form of a booklet containing nine parts and a blank page for an essay response. The various parts cover the different kinds of courses at Princeton, and students fill out only those which are applicable. Three of the parts are reprinted here.

Part 1: LECTURES

1. Applicable.............   Inapplicable.............

	Excel-lent	Good	Fair	Poor	Not Applic-able
2-11—*Rate the quality of the lectures in terms of the degree to which they:*					
2. Held your attention and interest	1	2	3	4	5 6 0
3. Covered the material at an appropriate intellectual level—neither too complicated nor too simple					
4. Clearly presented the relevant subject matter					
5. Covered diverse points of view and helped to expand your awareness of alternatives					
6. Emphasized principles and generalizations					
7. Stimulated your intellectual curiosity and provoked independent thinking					
8. Stimulated student discussion outside of class					
9. Were related to one another and followed a coherent sequence					
10. Were coordinated with other parts of the course					
11. Rate the general quality of the lectures as a whole					

12. In comparison to all other lecturers you have had at Princeton, how would you rate the lecturer in this course?

13. About how many lectures did you miss?
    1) 1 or more
    2) 2-4
    3) 5-7
    4) 8 or more

Category	A / B / C	D / E / F / G	H / I / J
4. Liberal and Progressive Attitude	4A 4B 4C — Welcomes differences in viewpoint.	4D 4E 4F 4G — Biased on some things but usually tolerant.	4H 4I 4J — Entirely intolerant, allows no contradiction.
5. Presentation of Subject Matter	5A 5B 5C — Clear, definite and forceful.	5D 5E 5F 5G — Sometimes mechanical and monotonous.	5H 5I 5J — Indefinite, involved, and monotonous.
6. Sense of Proportion and Humor	6A 6B 6C — Always keeps proper balance; not over-critical or over-sensitive.	6D 6E 6F 6G — Fairly well balanced.	6H 6I 6J — Over-serious; no sense of relative values.
7. Self-reliance and Confidence	7A 7B 7C — Always sure of himself; meets difficulties with poise.	7D 7E 7F 7G — Fairly self-confident; occasionally disconcerted.	7H 7I 7J — Hesitant, timid, uncertain.
8. Personal Peculiarities	8A 8B 8C — Wholly free from annoying mannerisms.	8D 8E 8F 8G — Moderately free from objectionable peculiarities.	8H 8I 8J — Constantly exhibits irritating mannerisms.
9. Personal Appearance	9A 9B 9C — Always well groomed; clothes neat and clean.	9D 9E 9F 9G — Usually somewhat untidy; gives little attention to appearance.	9H 9I 9J — Slovenly; clothes untidy and ill-kept.
10. Stimulating Intellectual Curiosity	10A 10B 10C — Inspires students to independent effort; creates desire for investigation.	10D 10E 10F 10G — Occasionally inspiring; creates mild interest.	10H 10I 10J — Destroys interest in subject; makes work repulsive.

Source: Copyright 1950 The Purdue Research Foundation, Purdue University. Developed by H. H. Remmers and D. N. Elliott.

THE PURDUE RATING SCALE FOR INSTRUCTION

Note to Students: Following is a list of factors which are important to many courses but over which the instructor often has little control. You are asked to rate the course on each of the factors by selecting one of the letters and write in space at the right of each statement.

If the course is *extremely poor* with respect to the factor write E in space.

If the course is *below average* with respect to the factor write D in space.

If the course is *average* with respect to the factor write C in space.

If the course is *above average* with respect to the factor write B in space.

If the course is *excellent* with respect to the factor write A in space.

For example: If you feel that the course is not contributing very much to the attainment of your ultimate goal; but on the other hand, is not a complete waste of time you would probably respond to item number 20 by writing D in space.

11. Suitability of the method or methods by which subject matter of the course is presented (recitation, lecture, laboratory, etc.) ....

12. Suitability of the size of the class (consider the subject matter and type of class—lecture, lab, etc.) ....

13. The degree to which the objectives of the course were clarified and discussed ....

14. The agreement between the announced objectives of the course and what was actually taught ....

15. Suitability of the reference materials available for the course ....

16. Suitability of the laboratory facilities available for the course ....

17. Suitability of the assigned textbook ....

18. The use made of tests as aids to learning ....

19. Amount of freedom allowed students in the selection of the materials to be studied (considering the subject matter) ....

20. How the course is fulfilling your needs (consider your ultimate as well as your immediate goals) ....

21. Range of ability in the class (are there too many extremely dull or extremely bright students?) ....

22. Suitability of the amount and type of assigned outside work ....

23. The weight given to tests in determining the final grade for the course ....

24. Coordination of the tests with the major objectives of the course ....

25. Frequency of tests ....

26. The overall rating of the instructor ....

Form 8.

COURSE EVALUATION

Note: The course evaluation questionnaire (which is copyrighted by Princeton University) is in the form of a booklet containing nine parts and a blank page for an essay response. The various parts cover the different kinds of courses at Princeton, and students fill out only those which are applicable. Three of the parts are reprinted here.

Part 1: LECTURES

1. Applicable............   Inapplicable............

	Excel-lent	Good	Fair	Poor	Not Applic-able

2-11—*Rate the quality of the lectures in terms of the degree to which they:*

2. Held your attention and interest	1	2	3	4	5	6	0

3. Covered the material at an appropriate intellectual level—neither too complicated nor too simple

4. Clearly presented the relevant subject matter

5. Covered diverse points of view and helped to expand your awareness of alternatives

6. Emphasized principles and generalizations

7. Stimulated your intellectual curiosity and provoked independent thinking

8. Stimulated student discussion outside of class

9. Were related to one another and followed a coherent sequence

10. Were coordinated with other parts of the course

11. Rate the general quality of the lectures as a whole

12. In comparison to all other lecturers you have had at Princeton, how would you rate the lecturer in this course?

13. About how many lectures did you miss?
    1) 1 or more
    2) 2-4
    3) 5-7
    4) 8 or more

14-22—*Often some very concrete characteristics of the lecturer reduce the value of a course or interfere with the achievement of its objectives. For each of the following characteristics indicate whether or not you felt that it applied to the lecturer:*

14. Inaudible   1   2   3   4   5   6
15. Writing illegible
16. Too abstract
17. Too superficial
18. Covers too much material
19. Speaks too fast
20. Disorganized presentations
21. Repetitious
22. Distracting mannerisms

(Specify: ....

....)

Which lectures (or lectures on what subjects) did you find least valuable? Why?

Part 3: PRECEPTS OR CLASSES

34. Applicable............ Inapplicable............

	Excellent	Good	Fair	Poor	Not Applicable

35-44—*Rate the general quality of the precepts or classes on each of the following: (The word instructor is used to refer to the person responsible for your section regardless of whether it was a class or a precept.)*

35. Interest of the instructor in the precept (class)
36. Instructor's ability to raise challenging questions
37. Instructor's ability to help clarify readings and lectures
38. Instructor's ability to encourage broad student participation
39. Instructor's ability to conduct discussions
40. Instructor's responsiveness to students' comments and questions
41. Integration with other parts of the course—relevant and supplementary
42. General attitude and preparedness of fellow class members
43. Your own interest, preparation and participation

44. Value of the precepts or classes   1   2   3   4   5   6   0
as a whole to this course

45. How many precepts or classes
did you miss?
  1) 1 or none
  2) 2-3
  3) 4-5
  4) 6 or more

Were there characteristics of the precepts (classes) which you found particularly valuable or not very useful? Please explain and, if possible, suggest modifications.

Name of Instructor: ....

Part 8: OVERALL RATINGS (Applicable To All Courses)

In relation to your own objectives in this course and compared to other courses you have taken at Princeton, how would you rate this course in terms of how much it contributed to each of the following:

	Excel-lent	Good	Fair	Poor	Not Applic-able
91. Your mastery of the relevant content or subject matter					
92. Your mastery of the relevant skills or methods					
93. Your ability to see more alternatives and have more insight into the complexity of the relevant subject matter					
94. Your ability to formulate general principles in the relevant subject matter					
95. Your abilities for critical evaluation in the relevant subject matter					
96. An increase in your interest in the field so as to take further related courses or do reading on your own					
97. An impact upon your emotional sensitivity to the relevant phenomena or upon your values and attitudes towards parts of life or yourself					
98. Your total educational growth and development					

Please write in below any generally descriptive comments you would like to make about the course or specific points which were not brought out in the questionnaire.

Form 9.

SURVEY OF STUDENT OPINION OF TEACHING
UNIVERSITY OF WASHINGTON

Instructor's Name ....

Course and Number ....

My major is ....

This course is required .... elective .... (check one)

My cumulative GPA is:

Below 2.5 .... 2.5 to 3.0 .... 3.0 to 3.5 .... above 3.5 ....

This survey is made at the request of your instructor in this class. The information the instructor receives will not identify any student individually. He will receive a summary of class ratings and comments only after the quarter is over. At that time the individual instructor alone determines whether this information is to be destroyed or whether it is to be made available to any other person for reference.

Listed below are several qualities which describe aspects of instructor behavior. Rate your instructor on each of these items by drawing a circle around the number that best indicates his position in comparison with other teachers you have had. Rate each item as thoughtfully and carefully as possible. Do *not* omit items. Of course, it will be the very unusual case when the number you write in is the same for all items.

Legend: (1) Outstanding. (2) Superior. (3) Competent. (4) Only Fair. (5) Of Less Value.

1. Interprets abstract ideas and theories   1   2   3   4   5
   clearly ....
2. Gets me interested in his subject ..
3. Has increased my skills in thinking
4. Has helped broaden my interests ..
5. Stresses important material ......
6. Makes good use of examples and illustrations ....
7. Has motivated me to do my best work ....
8. Inspires class confidence in his knowledge of subject ....
9. Has given me new viewpoints or appreciations ....
10. Is clear and understandable in his explanations ....

Your instructor would like to know if there is something you believe he has done especially well in the teaching of this course ....

....

....

Your instructor would also like to know what specific things you believe might be done to improve his teaching in this course ....

....

....

Thus far your judgments have been restricted to characteristics of the *teacher* himself. For the item below indicate your feeling for the *subject matter* of the course by checking the appropriate entry.

The subject matter or content of the course is:

Highly interesting ....
Moderately interesting ....
Not very interesting ....

Circle the final grade you expect to receive in this course: A B C D E

Legend: (1) *Outstanding.* (2) *Superior.* (3) *Competent.* (4) *Only Fair.* (5) *Of Less Value.*

11. Lectures gave viewpoints and info   1   2   3   4   5
    text did not contain ....
12. Material enthusiastically presented
    in lectures ....
13. Material presented in a well-orga-
    nized fashion ....
14. Helpful to individual students ....
15. Integration of material into coher-
    ent whole was ....
16. Text clear in presentation of concepts
17. Text's overall rating ....
18. How much was your interest in the subject changed by this course?
         More interested 1   2   3   4   5   Less interested
19. What level of student sophistication was assumed in lectures?
              Very high 1   2   3   4   5   Very low
20. Were students free to ask questions, disagree, express their ideas, etc.?
            Encouraged 1   2   3   4   5   Discouraged
21. Has improved my problem-solving methods.
             Very much 1   2   3   4   5   Not at all
22. Did test questions cover the material emphasized in the text and lectures?
             Very well 1   2   3   4   5   Very poorly
23. Would you recommend this course by this instructor to majors in this dept.?
           Very highly 1   2   3   4   5   Never
24. Would you recommend this course by this instructor to non-majors?
           Very highly 1   2   3   4   5   Never

Additional questions will be on the chalkboard if the instructor wants to use them. *Students were also asked to give class, age, sex, and expected grade in course.*

COURSE EVALUATION QUESTIONNAIRE

The major instructor of this course is:

The name and number of this course is:

....

....

(no.)   (name)

Your expected grade in this course: A, B, C, D, F

Are you: Fresh, Soph, Junior, Senior, Grad, Other

Are you taking this course for: Pass/Fail, Required/Elective

This course is within your: Major, Minor, Other

You are: Male, Female

Grade the following:

    The content of the course: A, B, C, D, F

    The major instructor: A, B, C, D, F

    The course in general: A, B, C, D, F

Response code:

    SA *Strongly Agree* with the item

    A *Agree* moderately with the item

    D *Disagree* moderately with the item

    SD *Strongly Disagree* with the item

1. I would take another course that was taught this way. ....

2. The instructor seemed to be interested in students as persons. .. ..

3. I would have preferred another method of teaching in this course. ....

4. It was easy to remain attentive. ....

5. The instructor did NOT synthesize, integrate or summarize effectively. ....

6. NOT much was gained by taking this course. ....

7. The instructor encouraged the development of new viewpoints and appreciations. ....

8. I learn more when other teaching methods are used. ....

9. The course material seemed worthwhile. ....

10. The instructor was excellent. ....

11. Homework assignments were helpful in understanding the course. ....

12. The instructor demonstrated a thorough knowledge of his subject matter. ....

13. The types of test questions used were good. ....

14. I would rather NOT take another course from this instructor. ....

15. It was a very worthwhile course. ....

16. Some things were NOT explained very well. ....

17. The course material was too difficult. ....

18. One of my poorest courses. ....

19. The instructor seemed to consider teaching as a chore or routine activity. ....

20. It was quite interesting. ....

21. I think that the course was taught quite well. ....

22. Excellent course content. ....

23. Some days I was NOT very interested in this course. ....

24. It was quite boring. ....

25. Overall, the course was good. ....

26. (Optional items) ....

Course Content:

Please give your comments on the course content, subject matter, and any particular relevance this course has had to your area of study.

Instructors:

Write the name of your principal instructor ....

T.A. ....

What are your general comments about the instructor(s) in this course?

Instructional Objectives:

Were the instructional objectives clearly stated for this course?

Yes............   No............

Comment: ....

....

Papers and Homework:

Comment on the value of books, homework, and papers (if any) in this course.

....

....

Exams:

Comment on the exams (quizzes, practicals) as to difficulty, fairness, etc.

General:

1. What improvements in this course would you suggest?
2. Please give your thoughtful evaluation of this course with comments.

Are you satisfied with what you got out of this course? Do you consider it a valuable educational experience? Simply a means of passing a requirement? Or a disappointment? Please comment.

Source: © The Board of Trustees of the University of Illinois, 1972. Further information available from Measurement and Research Division, 307 Engineering Hall, University of Illinois, Urbana, Illinois 61801.

marks the class number and session on the envelope, and delivers the envelope straight away to the designated office—probably the dean's office or the office for institutional research. A short turnaround time for the results of the rating forms—one or two weeks—verifies the administration's interest in using the results for positive purposes.

Correlates of Student Evaluations

Whenever student evaluations of faculty are discussed, certain issues invariably arise—in particular, the relationship of these student ratings to student achievement or grades; to student class level; to the teacher's personality, rank, age, and sex; to class size; and to the influence of feedback. Some additional issues, usually of less general interest, are worth some attention: the influence on ratings of the time of day, and of required versus elective courses, and the impact of student-conducted and student-published documents on classroom performance of teachers. The Bibliography should be consulted for additional references.

Achievement and grades. Some critics of faculty evaluation have contended that student ratings are directly related to grades given—the higher the grade the higher the ratings. And some research evidence supports this view, such as the study by Kennedy (1972), in which he cites similar conclusions by Weinstein and Bramble (1971) and the earlier work by Anikeeff (1953). Based on 16,000 analyzed student forms for classes of 406 teachers at the State College of Washington, Downie (1952) reported that only one item—how well course objectives were met—was rated less favorably by above 3.0 students, and twelve of the items were rated less favorably by those below 3.0.

The substantial number of studies, however, support the conclusion that no significant relationship exists between course grades, achievement, or grade point average and student course ratings. One suspects, along with Costin, and others (1971), that "the positive findings that do occur might be better viewed as a partial function of the better achieving students' greater interest and motivation, rather than as a mere contamination of the validity of student ratings." A study by Mueller and Miller (1970) did find a significant relationship among motivation, attitude toward course, hours of study on the course, and grades received. Holmes (n.d.) using 97 students in an introductory psychology course, sought to determine the effects of disconfirmed grade expectancies on students' evaluations of their instructor. One-half of the students who deserved and expected "A's" or "B's" were given their expected grades while one-half were given a grade one step lower than expected. After receiving the grades, the students filled out the Teaching Assessment Blank. A two-by-two analysis of variance revealed no difference in the evaluations as a function of differences in grades but evaluations on eleven of the nineteen items were lowered as a function of the unexpected lowering of grades. It was concluded that although differences in actual grades do not affect evaluations, if students' grades disconfirm their expectancies, the students will tend to deprecate the instructor's teaching performance in areas other than his grading system.

Class level. Do upperclassmen or graduate students rate teachers higher than underclassmen do? The findings on this question are mixed. Eckert and Keller (1954) and Miller (1972) found that seniors and graduate students rated courses higher than undergraduates; Gage (1961) found that teachers of lower-level courses were rated lower than the more advanced ones; Bendig (1952) found that upperclassmen were more unfavorable than lower classmen; and Detchen (1940) and Hildebrand (1971) found negligible differences in student ratings among the various grade levels. In view of this inconclusive picture, one can pretty much take either position. While the course ratings may not vary much between lower- and upper-division students, the additional comments written in the space provided on most rating forms may be more helpful as students mature with the collegiate experience and have a greater number of teachers as basis for their judgment; but, on the other hand, the numerous rating forms completed by the senior year may dull the student's interest in providing fresh and thoughtful comments.

A teacher personality. To what extent is the teacher's personality reflected in the students' ratings? Does an outgoing, gregarious teacher have higher ratings than a more introspective, reserved teacher? In his extensive research on teacher effectiveness, Ryans (1967) identified three personality patterns or behaving styles: Pattern X—friendly, understanding, sympathetic teacher behavior; Pattern Y—responsible, businesslike, systematic teacher behavior; and Pattern Z—stimulating, imaginative teacher behavior.

A number of studies have investigated the relationship between types of teacher personality and student ratings, and in general a significant relationship has not been established. Isaacson and others (1963) sought to determine whether five personality factors generally described as relevant traits to teaching—surgency, agreeableness, dependability, emotional stability, and culture— correlated with effective college teaching; and he found the only high correlation (0.48) was between the peer rating of culture and student rating of effectiveness. Based on his investigation, Lewis (1964) concluded that effective teachers cannot be differentiated from less effective ones on the basis of personality variables.

To what extent is showmanship or entertainment related to good grades? Guthrie (1954) found that "an examination of the names of the 62 teachers in the top decile of the annual ratings revealed a certain outgiving interest not unlike the interest of an actor or musician, coupled with a friendly interest in students as persons, and, most important, an industry and interest in the subject that insures his own preparation for every class period." Does the entertainment argument express a particular philosophical point of view? Does it not imply that learning is masochistic and students should receive education rather than experience learning? One effective teacher, for instance, was labeled a chemistry teacher. He would come into the laboratory and ask, "How are the molecules today?" He was entertaining because he believed in his subject and thoroughly enjoyed it, and he believed in his students and imparted to them much more than a knowledge of chemistry. The entertainment influence, therefore, may be difficult to separate from good teaching.

While research evidence supports the generalization made two paragraphs earlier, many questions remain unanswered: To what extent do students understand personality differences and make a knowing judgment on this basis, or what is the role of intuition? How do students' personalities affect the ratings they give, and how do basic personality differences between students and teachers affect student ratings? What magnitude of personality clash is likely to influence student ratings and what is not? These and other questions need further clarification and have had little research to date.

Teaching rank, age, experience. Common sense would have full professors ranked highest by students and instructors lowest, based on the logic that degrees and experience do make a difference, and age is related directly to degrees and experience. As with many common sense observations, however, the truth differs from the obvious—although only moderately so. An early study (Heilman and Armentrout, 1936) found no significant differences in student ratings given the same teachers over a five- to seven-year period; in fact, the teachers showed a slight decrease in the latter ratings. No reliable differences were reflected in the ratings of teachers who differed from five to twenty or more years in their teaching experience. Downie (1952) found no differences in student ratings at the State College of Washington between the under- and over-40 age groups, although full professors ranked the highest in student-teacher relations and teachers with the two highest degrees had better organized courses, more effective presentations, gave more appropriate assignments, knew their subject better, and stimulated intellectual curiosity better than those with only the bachelor's degree. On the other hand, Guthrie (1954) found no relationship between experience and teaching effectiveness, and slight improvement in ratings from one rank to another; but Goodhartz (1948) found that when students rated by age, they clearly placed the 20-39 age group ahead of the 40-49 and 50-69 groups with the exception of one trait—knowledge of subject. And Centra (1972) reported that the more experienced teachers were rated no better than those in their first or second years of teaching; in fact, on informing students of how they would be evaluated in the course, the more experienced teachers were rated less favorably.

The evidence currently available precludes generalizing about relationships between teaching rank and age/experience and student ratings of teaching. It may be that enthusiasm and newer knowledge among younger faculty members in the lower academic ranks offset the gains of experience and advanced degrees. Some professors may "peak out" in the early forties and coast along—at least for a while. For years, one struggles: first for the degree, then the rank and tenure, but by 40 or shortly thereafter has "everything." Unless he is self-energizing or the institution has developed a defined and operational system for faculty renewal, the over-40 professor may not have the incentives to strive for constant improvement and new learning. This speculative comment merely points up the inadequacy of the research base on this matter.

Size of class. Perceptions about class size are closely related to the size and style of the institution. If students are reminded frequently of the virtues of small classes, as are administrators and faculty in small colleges, one should not be surprised to find them favoring and therefore rating smaller classes better than larger classes, in the belief that small-class instruction is more personalized and therefore more effective (Gage, 1961; Miller, 1972). On the other hand, Goodhartz' Brooklyn College study (1948) found that classes of fewer than 20 students do not necessarily result in a more favorable teacher rating than those over 20; and Guthrie (1954) found little, if any, relationship between size of class and ratings given.

The evidence is far from conclusive and several other factors enter into the research findings, such as different styles of teaching for classes of 20 and 200, student expectations, the subject matter (science labs are planned for 20–30), and the disposition of college students to feel more comfortable in the class size range of 20 to 35 students because 12 years of elementary-secondary school experience has ingrained this expectation.

Influence of feedback. Do results of student evaluation improve teaching performance? This question is raised frequently by faculty members, and evidence is not plentiful. Again, logic would say "yes," but more analysis is necessary. The Baldwin-Wallace study (Miller, 1972) involved 2750 completed student appraisal forms, with a first test early in the quarter and a second one near the end. The product moment correlation of $+.68$ with significance at the .01 level indicates that the evaluation form (the one for student appraisal in the first book) had fairly good test-retest reliability. The overall rating score for professors by students was 59.20 on the first test and 61.43 on the second one. The 2.23 improvement may reflect instructional improvement although a direct cause-and-effect relationship cannot be established. Wilson (1932) reported that University of Washington teachers who systematically tried to correct weaknesses described by student ratings were raised 25 percentile points in a rating by another group of students after five months. On the other hand, M. Miller (1971) assigned 36 teaching assistants in three freshman courses at the University of Iowa to groups based on an attitude scale regarding the value they ascribe to student ratings. Instructors in feedback or attitude groups did not differ significantly on their end-of-semester ratings by students from those who did not have access to the ratings. Nonsignificant differences existed between the instructors' final ratings, as a function of their attitudes toward the value of the ratings; and for the instructors in two of the three courses, feedback from students' ratings did not improve instruction and hence the academic performance of the students. Centra (1972) conducted a five-college study with over 400 teachers to investigate the effects of feedback from student ratings on changing instructional practices, using three groups: feedback, no-feedback, or posttest. Multivariate analysis of variance results for the end-of-semester ratings indicated no significant differences among the three groups. A major hypothesis of the study, however, was that student feedback would effect changes in instructors who rated themselves more favorably than their students had rated them. Results of the regression analyses indicated this; the results suggested that the greater the discrepancy—where the discrepancy reflected the extent to which students rated teachers less favorably than the teachers apparently expected—the greater the likelihood of change. Some additional evidence (Bryan, 1966; Comaford, 1954; Remmers, 1959; Tuckman and Oliver, 1968) indicates a positive influence of student ratings on the quality of classroom instruction. In sum, one can say that a relationship does seem to exist between student ratings and instructional improvement, but more research is needed on this important matter. And several other factors need to be investigated, such as the teacher's attitude toward student evaluation, the level of effectiveness of the teacher, the experience of the teacher with the particular course, and the type of course (lecture or discussion)'.

Sex. A number of studies have investigated differences in teaching evaluation made by male and female students, and differences in student ratings of male and female teachers. The studies substantially find no significant differences in terms of the sex of the student or that of the teacher. Again, some evidence is to the contrary: Bendig (1952) found that female students were more unfavorable than males in their ratings; McKeachie, and others (1971) found that female teachers rated high in structure were rated more effective than their male counterparts; and Downie (1952) reported that female teachers were rated more favorably on the use of new materials. Centra's research (1972) found that female teachers were more likely to know when students did not know the material, were more concerned with student progress, made more comments on papers or examinations, and generally made better use of class time. Courses taught by male teachers were rated more stimulating and more difficult.

While one can be reasonably confident that no significant differences exist in teaching ratings based on the sex of the rater or the teacher, many questions remain unanswered: Do ratings based on sex vary according to discipline; do they vary in different types of institutions, and do they reveal different teaching styles of female and male teachers, and is age a factor?

Required and elective courses. Several studies have compared student ratings made for required with those made for elective courses, and the findings substantially agree that no significant differences exist between student ratings on required and elective courses. Some evidence does exist to the contrary, however. Gage (1961) found that teachers of elective courses had higher ratings than did instructors of required courses.

Time of day. Do those who begrudgingly meet the day with a professor at 8:00 A.M. take the hour out on the professor? According to Eckert and Keller (1954), classes held during the mid-portion of the day received higher ratings than early morning ones. Additional research is needed to verify or modify the conclusion, since the finding has some importance. We need to know if students' instructional ratings vary according to the time of day; and the analysis should consider other factors such as whether those teachers lower on the academic totem pole, the young assistant professors, usually end up with the earlier classes.

Student-Administered Systems

Beginning in the mid-1960s and continuing through 1971, many student-initiated and operated systems of faculty evaluation came into being. As rapidly as this movement developed, it has receded. Spurred by the student movement and general student dissatisfaction with instructional quality, students developed their own ratings systems, administered, collected, evaluated, and published the results. In some cases the documents were noted for their fairness and sensitivity, but others were hastily compiled and unfairly critical. A few lawsuits were filed by professors who believed their professional reputations were damaged by inadequate student rating systems. Student groups planning to conduct their own evaluation of teaching should consult with professors or administrators beforehand. It is better to have the faculty-administration conduct such evaluations because the natural turnover in student leadership makes difficult the necessary continuity and stability. Also, cost factors, professional experience, and institutional perspective are factors. Some administrators, however, have planted the idea of faculty evaluation among student leaders as to spur the faculty, believing that the faculty would prefer their own rather than a student-controlled system.

4

Case Study of
Teacher Evaluation

The dilemma of faculty evaluation is succinctly characterized by the following statement of assumed adequacy: administrators "ask for evidence of scholarly competence but assume teaching competence. And students ask for evidence of teaching competence but assume scholarly competence (Hammond, Meyer, and Miller, 1971)." When the ambivalence suggested by this statement is coupled with an uncertain and frequently nondiscriminating reward structure, frustrations associated

This chapter is by Richard Fenker, associate professor, and Leigh Secrest, vice-chancellor for advanced studies and research, Texas Christian University. Secrest served as chairman of the committee which designed and conducted the evaluation program discussed in this chapter. The chapter, to a large extent, represents a report of the committee's work and hence, credit for much of the material presented must be given to the committee as a whole rather than the two authors. Committee members included the co-authors, Herbert LaGrone, James Newcomer, Frank Reuter, John Hitt, Marjorie Lewis, Anne Lane, Michael Winesanker, James Whinnery, David Hall, Paul Wassenich, and Joe Enochs. The authors wish to acknowledge the invaluable assistance of Edwin Cornelius, a doctoral student at TCU, who was responsible for the data analyses reported in this chapter.

with tight academic budgets, and the absence of definitive measures for evaluating the many complex aspects of faculty behavior, the cautious outlook of many faculty and administrators toward evaluation programs can be understood. An awareness of these difficulties nevertheless does not greatly mollify the administrator faced with the practical problem of disbursing rewards or the faculty member who demands that his achievements be recognized and rewarded. Cognizant of many of the pitfalls associated with evaluation procedures, yet pressed by practical needs, Texas Christian University decided to implement an experimental evaluation program. This paper discusses the issues that were considered in designing the program and presents data on the roles of faculty as perceived by various groups within the university.

Evaluation Program

As a result of a self-study program, suggestions from university advisory groups, and impetus provided by the chancellor, TCU embarked on a full-scale evaluation program during the spring of 1971. The program was intended to meet the following needs or goals: (1) to improve the overall quality of the university by providing an objective means for evaluating its personnel, suggesting improvements or changes, and distributing rewards on the basis of a sufficiently complex definition of excellence; (2) to acknowledge the importance of excellent teaching and to implement this conviction in the university's reward structure; (3) to reduce the arbitrariness of the decision-making processes associated with tenure, promotions, and raises by making the reward structure more explicit; (4) to recognize the diversification of behaviors that constitute excellence for a faculty member or administrator and to establish criteria for evaluating these behaviors.

A university committee consisting of students, faculty, and administrators was appointed to develop evaluation instruments and if possible conduct a trial run of the evaluation procedures during the 1971-1972 academic year. Much of the material in the current paper is based on the work of this committee. The paper is divided into two major sections. The first contains a description of the activities of the committee in planning, developing, and implementing the evaluation program. The second presents the results of a validation study intended to provide feedback from faculty, students, and administrators on the suitability of the evaluation instruments. The validation data were used to investigate differences in the perceptions of the various subgroups within the university community.

Questionnaire development. It was the committee's original intention to develop instruments for upward, downward, and parallel evaluation of faculty and administrators. At the time these instruments were designed, it was anticipated the upward evaluation of faculty, the teacher evaluation, would meet the most resistance. This hunch could not have been more wrong. The committee constructed instruments for teacher evaluation (faculty by students), colleague evaluation (faculty by faculty), self-evaluation, evaluation of professional staff, and evaluation of the state of the university. Each questionnaire had a different set of guidelines; however, the current paper concerns only the teacher evaluation and the colleague evaluation.

The teacher evaluation questionnaire was developed primarily on the basis of other successful questionnaires, particularly the one constructed at the Davis campus of the University of California (Hildebrand and Wilson, 1971). The individual items on the questionnaire were divided into six categories, five of which represented the following scales: analytic-synthetic approach; organization-clarity; instructor-group interaction; instructor-individual student interaction; dynamism-enthusiasm. The sixth category contained questions related to specific mechanical details of the course. Most of the questions included in the questionnaire had in previous research discriminated significantly between good and poor teachers.

The colleague evaluation instrument was designed to measure the variety of activities that characterize faculty behavior at an institution such as TCU. The major categories of faculty behavior were: (1) teaching: classroom and interactions with individual students; (2) research: current activity, creativity, reputation; (3) participation in university activities: committee assignments, role in campus organizations; (4) administrative responsibilities; (5) outside professional activities: consulting, serving as a reviewer, public speaking.

A number of the individual items associated with the first

three categories were selected because in the Davis study (Hildebrand and Wilson, 1971) they were shown to discriminate between good and poor teachers.

Political considerations. It was apparent to the committee that any attempt to implement a project with the scope and potential impact of a full-scale evaluation program would generate considerable discussion and controversy, especially in a freedom-oriented university setting. Before any of the details of the proposed evaluation procedures were distributed to the university community, an attempt was made to anticipate the problems or issues likely to be raised. On the basis of these political considerations the following ideas were stressed in publicizing the evaluation program:

(1) The privacy of individuals would be protected. Public distribution of teacher evaluations would not be allowed without permission of the faculty member involved.

(2) The evaluation procedures were regarded as experimental. Both the form of the instruments and details concerning their implementation were not in any sense fixed, but were to be be decided on the basis of feedback from the university community.

(3) It was noted that evaluation was currently taking place at all levels in the university, and that the purpose of the evaluation instruments was to "make more objective and explicit the processes of evaluation already at work in the university and to provide a process of gathering a more complete range of information concerning faculty members and administrators in their work."

(4) Open hearings on the evaluation procedure were held by the faculty senate with the evaluation committee answering questions and recording suggestions for changes.

(5) The validation study (to be described below) gave each individual faculty member and administrator the chance to comment on the questionnaires in a constructive (or nonconstructive) manner and insured that if job requirements or teaching styles differed across departments or other divisions of the university, this diversity would be noted.

(6) Considerable attention was given to matters of protocol. Representatives of various student and faculty groups were kept informed of the committee's activities. Traditional lines of com-

munication (proper channels) were utilized in distributing and collecting information associated with the evaluation procedure.

Validation Procedure

Although some questionnaire items were validated on the basis of previous research, many were not because of the difficulty of finding external criteria related to all of the behaviors being evaluated. In many cases, the behaviors described on the evaluation questionnaires represent the most meaningful criteria for defining outstanding performance. Also, since it was anticipated that the patterns of behavior that characterize expected performance might differ across departments, some type of face-validation study was deemed necessary to collect information on these differences.

The validation study was therefore intended to provide information on the perceived relevance of the items on the various questionnaires to differentiate between the various university groups, and to validate the individual items by demonstrating that their importance was commonly agreed on. Also it served as a communication device, informing the university community of the nature of the proposed program and providing opportunity for participation. Students, faculty, and administrators were sent copies of all the evaluation instruments and asked to rate each item in terms of its importance or relevance for the position being evaluated. Thus, both students and faculty rated the importance of groups. With the exception of a study by Field, Simpkins, Browne, and Rich (1971), discriminant analysis procedures have not been used in the evaluation area.

Teacher evaluation questionnaire. MDA techniques were used to investigate the differences between student, faculty, and administrator responses to the teacher evaluation questionnaire. The three groups agreed mostly on the importance of the various criteria defining good teaching. Despite this general agreement, however, three significant discriminant axes (dimensions of difference) were found.

The first axis represented a general dimension with almost all questionnaire items having moderate or high projections. An item's projection on a discriminant axis is analogous to its correlation[1] with that axis. The items with large projections on a particular discriminant axis are items on which the various groups differed in their importance ratings; hence these items represent the set of related criteria which determines the meaning of the axis. When all items have moderate or high loadings on a particular axis, this indicates that there were differences in the mean ratings of groups irrespective of the nature of the items. The first discriminant axis for the teacher-evaluation questionnaire reveals that administrators and faculty generally gave higher importance ratings to *all* items than did the student groups.

The second axis discriminated between underclassmen (freshmen and sophomores) and all other groups (juniors, seniors, faculty, and administrators). This dimension represented the instructor's enthusiasm or attention-getting ability. Items such as: "usually held your attention during class" and "revealed enthusiasm in his teaching" were highly correlated with the axis. Evidently, the underclassmen considered stimulating teachers to be more important than did the other groups.

The third axis was defined by items concerned with the mechanical details of the course rather than the instructor. Interestingly, freshmen rated these items considerably less important than did the other groups, while sophomores rated them considerably more important. As before, juniors, seniors, faculty, and administrators had similar ratings. This axis has several interesting interpretations best left to the reader's imagination.

While the results of the analysis of the teacher evaluation questionnaire are not terribly surprising, they do illustrate the potential usefulness of discriminant techniques in evaluation research. The analysis of the colleague evaluation questionnaire provides additional support.

Faculty colleague questionnaire. The faculty validation responses to the college questionnaire were divided by colleges into eight groups (Divinity, Business, Education, Fine Arts, Humanities,

[1] It is not necessarily true that item projections on discriminant axes represent correlation coefficients, however, in the present analyses the projections were normalized and thus have values ranging from -1.0 to $+1.0$.

Natural Sciences, Social Sciences, Nursing) and analyzed using a multiple discriminant procedure. The administrators represented a ninth group. The analysis yielded four significant discriminant axes which were interpreted as follows:[2]

Dimension 1: This is a bipolar dimension characterized on one pole by items that reflect the importance of research, and on the other by items that suggest a "good member of the university community" stereotype. Faculty groups who rated the dimension as highly important are concerned with university committees ("works well as a member of a committee"), are involved in student and faculty organizations, are interested in students, and are *not* especially interested in research. Faculty groups with low weights on the dimension rated the *good member* items as less important and the items related to research as highly important. This dimension is bipolar because it suggests that, at least at TCU, faculty fitting the *good member* stereotype are *not* especially concerned with research and vice-versa. Analysis of the various faculty groups' weights for this dimension revealed that the business school and school of education were high while the natural sciences were low.

Dimension 2: This concerns the breadth of the faculty ("seems well read beyond the subject he teaches"), their creativity, and their interest in teaching. The humanities have, by a considerable margin, the highest weight on this dimension followed by the divinity school and the administrators. The social sciences and the business school gave the lowest ratings for the items associated with this dimension.

Dimension 3: This axis clearly represents a local visibility dimension, since highly correlated items were: "has done work with which you are familiar;" "is an active participant in the affairs of the academic communities;" and "is recognized as an active citizen by the community." Groups with high weights were the divinity school, fine arts, social sciences, and the administrators. Although no group gave this dimension a low importance rating, by relative

[2] The results of this analysis must be regarded as tentative since three of the nine faculty groups had less than 50% return rate for the validation questionnaires. If there is a bias introduced by this sampling problem, it is likely to favor "community-oriented" individuals returning the questionnaires.

standards the natural sciences and the business school had the lowest scores.

Dimension 4: This dimension represents a national visibility axis and is defined by items such as: "is asked to serve as a consultant to other organizations;" and "has gained national or international recognition for his work." The Natural Sciences, Fine Arts, and Nursing have the highest weights on this dimension while the social sciences, the business school, the humanities, and the divinity school anchor the opposite end.

The MDA of the colleague questionnaire data substantiates an earlier prediction that different patterns of behavior are considered most appropriate in different departments or schools. The information derived would be extremely useful if the colleague instrument were used as part of an overall evaluation program.

Current state of project. The paper thus far has dealt with the more academic aspects of the evaluation program, the development of the instruments, and an analysis of the data obtained from the validation study. This is not the full story. As the reader might expect, the entire evaluation project, in particular the development of trial instruments and the validation procedures, engendered considerable discussion throughout the university community. Although much of the debate was constructive, the emotional overtones of many of these discussions made clear considerable disagreement between various groups in the university on whether there should be objective evaluation, who should evaluate whom, and what purposes an evaluation program could serve. The major issues seemed to be associated with the following points:

(1) By far the largest amount of criticism and emotion were directed at the colleague evaluation questionnaire. It was apparently a difficult instrument to complete because it required information that only a faculty member's closest colleagues would be capable of providing. Many people felt that implementing such procedure would be extremely bad for morale.

(2) Many faculty apparently prefer the subjective evaluation of an authority figure such as a chairman or dean to any kind of explicit, objective questionnaire. The possibility of appealing an unfavorable decision with the objective questionnaire data was not important.

(3) Several faculty groups felt that because they were not represented on the committee that developed the instruments, important considerations were ignored. The dissident groups were invited to send representatives to join the committee, and in fact, the individual from the business school raised some pertinent issues concerning the managerial implications of an evaluation system.

(4) One important argument against all the procedures was that they could do the faculty no good, but could cause harm. The faculty could not benefit from the evaluation program because the university budget was too tight to provide adequate rewards for outstanding performance; yet some reprisal could be taken against the faculty members who received low evaluations.

After a careful analysis of the data collected during the validation study and the information obtained from the senate hearings and later discussions, the committee decided to drop the colleague evaluation instrument and instead substitute a rating form to be completed by department chairman (and perhaps close associates)'. Eliminating the colleague questionnaire had an interesting effect on the overall evaluation program. There was little left in the way of opposition to the teacher evaluation or other evaluation instruments. This was a little surprising since previous attempts to implement a teacher evaluation procedure had not met with general acceptance by the faculty. Although it was not deliberately intended, the colleague questionnaire served as the "ape's hand" in the evaluation system.[3]

TCU completed (spring, 1972) a trial run of the entire evaluation procedure with little commotion or controversy. The success of the trial run and the previous success with the validation study probably depended on two important aspects of the evaluation program. First, the chancellor wanted the program developed. By providing the committee with both impetus and the necessary resources he made it possible for the committee's work to be effectively channeled through all levels of the university. The second important

[3] The ape's hand phenomenon refers to the behavior of an artist (historical reality unconfirmed) who painted for the Spanish aristocracy. Bothered by the fact that the king insisted on having one change made in each new portrait, the artist began painting an ape's hand into each picture. The moral is obvious.

consideration was that everyone, faculty, administrators, and professional staff were evaluated. This eliminated objections which might be raised from groups singled out for evaluation (at many other universities, only the faculty are evaluated). Will the evaluation program accomplish its intended goals? We do not know. At least it is possible to collect the data. One office is completely filled and things are very quiet.

5

Administrative
Evaluation

Effective management is the key to the success of any institutionalized enterprise. According to *Forbes* magazine (September 15, 1968, pp. 51–52), "the clear lesson of fifty action-packed years of U.S. business history" is: "If a company has nothing going for it except one thing—good management—it will make the grade. If it has everything except good management, it will flop." The generalization applies to universities as well, although the range is from success to poor quality because public universities do not "flop." The critical role of administration in institutional success makes some systematic evaluation desirable, and probably instrumental, in administrative improvement. Moreover, faculty members are increasingly asking: "Why evaluate just faculty members?" The stock answer, "We do not have effective procedures for administrative evaluation," begs the question: "Can not they be developed, and why not start now?"

Evaluation should include all segments of the collegiate enterprise: students, faculty, service personnel, administrators. We have a rich literature of research and experience in student and faculty evaluation, very little on service personnel, and still less on administrators. The latter categories will be discussed in this chapter.

A college president spends about one-quarter of his time on instructionally related activities, and this segment, difficult as it is, might be the easiest component to judge. But who judges the other three-quarters? The board of trustees has the final say, but from whom do they receive their information? And how about the academic dean? He is the man in the middle, the man in the swivel chair, the man without a constituency, and whatever else he has been called. (*Dean* is also a four-letter word—like *love, hate, work, stop, go-go!*) Is his effectiveness judged on short-term consequences rather than on long-term planning and programs that also are part of his responsibility?

Faculty evaluation—with all of its problems, complexities, and greynesses—is more solid, accurate, and sophisticated a procedure than any others we have for administrative evaluation. Yet the logic for administrative evaluation is compelling: If one segment of academia is to be evaluated, so should the others! The consideration of administration is further complicated by collective bargaining. The collective bargaining model is based on an antagonistic relationship (Finkin, 1971), yet evaluation should be done in a different spirit. We do not know the extent to which administrative evaluation in a collective bargaining model is realistic, but we should not assume that because collective bargaining exists, impartial and fair evaluation of administrators cannot take place.

Guidelines

A search of the literature for information on administrative evaluation turns up very little indeed, and three advertisements in *The Chronicle of Higher Education* added only a handful of examples. The literature does reveal, however, that elementary and secondary schools are ahead of colleges and universities. The Ohio Department of Elementary School Principals, for example, developed a booklet on *Evaluation of Administrators* (1971). (See Form 11.) The booklet contends that any appraisal using a structured instrument and systematic procedures should accomplish three primary goals: "(1) assist school administrators in developing sensitivity to their competencies; (2) identify general areas in be-

FORM 11.

EVALUATION SCALE FOR
ADMINISTRATIVE PERSONNEL
(Shaker Heights (Ohio) City School District)

CANDIDATE FOR EVALUATION: ....

....

	Performance Scale				
	Inade-quate		*Satis-factory*		*Out-standing*
I. *Exercise of Leadership*	5	4	3	2	1

   A. in total instructional program (or special field)

      1. as to knowledge of field(s)

      2. as to application of knowledge

   B. in general administration

II. *Exercise of Judgment*

   A. with other people

   B. with program, plant, etc.

III. *Dealing with Special Problems and Unique Characteristics of the Job Responsibility* (personnel, plant, equipment, etc.)

IV. *Practice of Cooperativeness Within the System and Concern for the General Welfare of the District*

V. *Skill in the Achievement of Desirable Public Relations*

   A. in particular relation to present responsibility

   B. in general on behalf of the entire system

FORM 11.

	Performance Scale				
	Inade-quate		*Satis-factory*		*Out-standing*
VI. *Continued Development of Profes-*sional Characteristics	5	4	3	2	1

     A. by effort made to be alert pro-fessionally

     B. by contributions to the profession

Evaluation completed by ....

         Date ....

havior, adequacies, and skills in which improvements are needed; (3) develop realistic job targets, both short- and long-range, to assist the professional growth of individual administrators."

Based on a study of the available literature, the following guidelines are suggested for administrative evaluation in higher education: (1) The evaluative system should be rooted in the traditions, purposes, and objectives of each college or university. (2) The overall purpose of the evaluative procedure should be to improve the quality of administration and its basic approach should be positive rather than punitive—as should be the case in faculty evaluation also. The procedure should be built on the belief that each administrator possesses different administrative abilities and skills, and the effort is the strengthen weaknesses. (3) Performance should be evaluated against expectations, which requires that job descriptions exist, are current, and are reasonably specific. Job descriptions that are more than two or three years old usually need considerable revision. (4) The procedures for evaluation should employ objective measures as well as subjective ones. (5) Evaluations should be sought from those in a position to make valid judgments, with immediate administrative superiors having the major responsibility. (6) Evaluation should take place with the evaluated's full knowledge of the procedures, timetable, and results. (7) Confidentiality should be maintained throughout, with distribution of results clearly understood and controlled.

Appraisal Procedures

Appraisal forms may be helpful in systematizing the overall process. Standardized forms are common in student and faculty evaluation, so there is no reason why they cannot be employed for administrators—except that they are largely nonexistent. But we do have some models, and any institution can construct its own objective measures. The University of Redlands has developed evaluation sheets for administrators. As described by James D. Hester, vice–president for administrative services (1972):

> The central feature of the evaluation is that it is carried on by two distinct groups of people: one by the superior involved with the person being evaluated, and secondly by the staff whom the person being evaluated supervises.
>
> In the first instance, the evaluation is carried out on the basis of a kind of 'management by objectives' approach. We are trying to develop a process whereby the top-level administrator sits down with middle-management people and helps them develop goals and objectives for their areas of responsibility and for themselves. Then having mutually agreed upon goals and objectives, the middle-management person is asked at the end of the year whether these goals and objectives have been met by his staff and by himself. Evaluation then can be somewhat more objective and not related to kinds of dress, length of hair, or political affiliations.
>
> The second-level evaluation is done by the people with whom the person being evaluated has to deal every day to meet goals and objectives. It may well be that he or she may ask their staffs, including the secretaries, to set objectives.
>
> But the purpose of allowing the staff to evaluate their supervisor is really to find out how that person comes across to the staff in helping them to become either better in their own jobs, or in the way they deal with others, or in the way they function in the total office community.

At this point, one might raise the matter of administrative style and taste. In theory, few object to having secretaries evaluate bosses, but in practice the matter can be more complicated. Is the boss who is a boss to be marked down because he is under pressures and deadlines? To what extent can he share confidential knowledge with secretaries who may be interrelated to faculty members? The whole matter of having service personnel evaluate administrators is virtually unexplored.

Catonsville Community College in Maryland conducts an annual survey of administrative services "to give the College faculty an opportunity to assess administrative services, to determine the extent to which the faculty has been informed on major institutional developments, to discover specific weaknesses of the methods used in providing services to faculty and students, and to determine specific faculty, student, and administrative needs which may not have been expressed formally." The 15-page, multiple-choice document, signed by the president, includes 58 questions as well as space for other comments. The survey ranges over such matters as working climate; your role in decision making in your unit; the conduct of meetings in your unit; styles of leadership; committee participation; availability, adequacy, and utilization of instructional media; use of library; selection process of new personnel; uses and effectiveness of counseling center, adequacy of student health service; participation in developing the budget; and the frequency of use of a number of intercampus communications.

Hillway (1973; see Form 12) writes that in view of the burgeoning influence of administration on the educational program and in light of recent public demands for accountability, attempts to evaluate the work of administrators more carefully and fairly seem to be in order. He has developed a rating scale of 15 qualities and nine methods or activities. Qualities are: interest in the progress of education, educational and cultural background, sympathetic attitude toward students, fairness in dealing with students, considerate attitude toward faculty, fairness in dealing with faculty, self-adjustment and sense of humor, tolerance of new ideas, trustworthiness (honesty, reliability), skill in securing group action, ability to inspire confidence, ability to organize, ability to maintain faculty morale, ability to maintain faculty performance, and appearance (dress and grooming). Methods are: encourages democratic participation, communicates effectively with group members, presents appropriate materials for group action, adheres faithfully to group decisions, respects professional rights of faculty, assigns work fairly and suitably, makes fair decisions on promotions and salary, makes contributions to his academic field, and uses appropriate administrative methods.

The University of Tennessee at Chattanooga has developed two administrative forms (see Form 13) : one for division directors and department chairmen which has an emphasis consonant with their academic-administrative roles, and another form for the college deans which is purely administrative. As explained by Jane W. Harbaugh, dean of arts and sciences (1972), "each level is evaluated by the one just above; using the respective forms but supplementing the bare bones of the form. In turn, each individual writes a personal evaluation. A conference is scheduled and these documents are exchanged, and additional comments are made if desired by either party. These face-to-face conferences are quite essential to the process. However, if an individual does not wish to review his evaluation in conference, he need not do so." *Evaluating Faculty Performance* contains a form for evaluating administrators (see Form 14).

Evaluation models from industry and business need to be studied for their applicability to higher education. Bekins Moving and Storage Company, for example, has developed (1970) an elaborate "management by objectives" approach (see Form 15) to allow evaluation of an employee's performance for salary increases, bonus consideration, and promotions. Over a period of years it summarizes an employee's career history at Bekins and a record of his accomplishments. The plan has three steps: setting objectives consonant with those of the company and unit, and having them approved; working toward these objectives which are stated in operational rather than general terms; and reviewing the results, or measuring accomplishments in terms of objectives. A performance appraisal report is also used (see Form 16), with the rater appraising the employees in his jurisdiction in nine categories on a four-point scale: quality of work, volume of work, personal work habits, adaptability, judgment, knowledge and skill, attitude, customer relations, and team-effort leadership. Three lines are available for each factor and "reasons must be given" for the ratings checked for each of the nine factors.

FORM 12.

RATING SCALE FOR ACADEMIC ADMINISTRATION

PART I

Directions: Following is a list of personal and professional *qualities* generally considered to be desirable in administrators of colleges and universities. To obtain information that may lead to the improvement of administration, you are asked to rate the indicated administrator on each of these qualities. On the basis of your own experience and judgment, rate the administrator as high, fairly high, moderate, fairly low, or low, in each quality by writing the quality on the line at the end of each sentence.

Administrator's Name and Title:

.... Date ....

1. Interest in the Progress of Education ....

2. Educational and Cultural Background ....

3. Sympathetic Attitude toward Students ....

4. Fairness in Dealing with Students ....

5. Considerate Attitude toward Faculty ....

6. Fairness in Dealing with Faculty ....

7. Self-adjustment and Sense of Humor ....

8. Tolerance of New Ideas ....

9. Trustworthiness (Honesty, Reliability) ....

10. Skill in Securing Group Action ....

11. Ability to Inspire Confidence ....

12. Ability to Organize ....

13. Ability to Evaluate Faculty Performance ....

14. Ability to Maintain Faculty Morale ....

15. Appearance (Appropriate Dress, Grooming) ....

PART II

Directions: Following is a list of activities that relate to the methods employed by the administrator in performing his or her administrative work. You are asked to rate the administrator on the relative degree to which you consider that he or she engages in these activities or applies these methods—high, fairly high, moderate, fairly low, low.

16. Encourages Democratic Participation ....

17. Communicates Effectively with Group Members ....

18. Presents Appropriate Materials for Group Action ....

19. Adheres Faithfully to Group Decisions ....

20. Respects Professional Rights of Faculty ....

21. Assigns Work Fairly and Suitably ....

22. Makes Fair Decisions on Promotions and Salary ....

23. Makes Contributions to His Academic Field ....

24. Uses Generally Appropriate Administrative Methods ....

25. Overall Rating of Administrator ....

Source: Copyright © 1972 by Tyrus Hillway, University of Northern Colorado, Greeley, Colorado, 80639.

In their article, "Positive Program for Performance Appraisal," Kindall and Gatza (1963) criticize typical company evaluation programs for becoming entangled in personality factors, for looking at causes rather than results, and for poorly defined and negative procedures. The authors outline a five-step program for the appraisal of executives, supervisory, sales, staff, and similar positions:

> Step 1: the individual discusses his job description with his superior and they agree on the content of his job and the relative importance of his major duties—the things he is paid to do and is accountable for.
> Step 2: the individual establishes performance targets for each of his responsibilities for the forthcoming period.
> Step 3: he meets with his superior to discuss his target program.

Text continued on Page 91

FORM 13.
ADMINISTRATIVE FORMS

DIVISION DIRECTORS AND DEPARTMENT CHAIRMEN

Name ....

Title ....

Department ....Appointment Date ....

Evaluation by ....

Exceptions ....

Noted by ....

Legend: (1) Outstanding. (2) Satisfactory. (3) Unsatisfactory. (4) Not applicable.

1. *Planning* (establishment of objectives and goals; anticipation of future developments; formulation of effective plans to achieve desired results) ....

2. *Decision Making* (ability to make sound, logical decisions under stress; exercise of good judgment; ability to see problems objectively) .. ..

3. *Provide leadership in:*
   a) developing professional responsibility for teaching and related duties ....
   b) developing departmental morale ....
   c) developing institutional loyalty ....
   d) professional development through study and research ....
   e) the departmental program for advising students ....

4. *Administration* (staffing, organization, handling problems, development of new and better methods, procedures, or ideas, implementation of committee assignments) ....

5. *Communicative Skills* (quality of reports and correspondence, listening ability, oral presentation, participation in discussions and meetings, methods used for flow of information) ....

6. *Initiative* (drive, self-starting ability, capacity to act promptly, a striving to attain goals, willingness to work beyond ordinary requirements, independent action) ....

7. *Adaptability* (reaction to new responsibilities, handling of special projects, attitude, flexibility) ....

8. *Institutional Commitment* (dedication to service, willingness to strive for superior quality performance, sense of responsibility, concern for welfare of total University as well as specific responsibilities, promotion of favorable public relations, involvement in appropriate campus activities) ....

DEANS

1. *Planning* (establishment of objectives and goals; anticipation of future developments; formulation of effective plans to achieve desired results) ....

2. *Decision Making* (ability to make sound, logical decisions under stress; exercise of good judgment; ability to see problems objectively) ....

3. *Effectiveness in Dealing with People* (leadership ability, ability to develop subordinates, cooperation with team, ability to present ideas and get them accepted) ....

4. *Administration* (execution of plans, staffing, organization, job accomplishment, handling problems, development of new and better methods, procedures, or ideas) ....

5. *Job Knowledge* (amount of job knowledge necessary to perform assigned duties and responsibilities and to accomplish stated objectives, specialized training, experience) ....

6. *Communicative Skills* (quality of reports and correspondence, listening ability, oral presentation, participation in discussions and meetings, methods used for flow of information) ....

7. *Initiative* (drive, self-starting ability, capacity to act promptly, a striving to attain goals, willingness to work beyond ordinary requirements, independent action) ....

8. *Adaptability* (reaction to new responsibilities, handling of special projects, attitude, flexibility) ....

9. *Professional Self-Improvement* (independent study and research, advanced degree program, related study at seminars or workshops, memberships and positions held in professional organizations, participation in professional studies and research, knowledge of current developments in field) ....

10. *Institutional Commitment* (dedication to service, willingness to strive for superior quality performance, sense of responsibility, concern for welfare of total University as well as specific responsibilities, promotion of favorable public relations, involvement in appropriate campus activities) ....

Source: Developed by F. I. Brownley, Jr., with assistance from Jane Harbaugh, University of Tennessee, Chattanooga.

FORM 14.

ADMINISTRATIVE EFFECTIVENESS APPRAISAL

Year ....

Name of Administrator ....

Appraiser ....

Title ....

Directions:

Write the number in the blank space that describes your judgment of that factor. Rate the administrator on each item that is appropriate, giving the highest scores for unusually effective performances. The blank numbers allow for two additional items, and the space at the end of the survey allows for a narrative description.

							Don't
Highest			*Average*			*Lowest*	*Know*
7	6	5	4	3	2	1	X

.... 1. Ability and willingness to "open doors" for faculty members.

.... 2. Attends to details effectively.

.... 3. Instills enthusiasm for professional goals.

.... 4. Judges people perceptively and fairly.

.... 5. Keeps abreast of new developments and innovations in higher education.

.... 6. Makes sound decisions.

.... 7. Plans effectively and imaginatively.

.... 8. Resolves or ameliorates human conflicts.

.... 9. Says "no" effectively.

.... 10. Understands and uses modern management procedures.

.... 11. Willingness to appraise situations and problems impartially.

.... 12. Willingness to put others first.

.... 13. Works effectively with faculty members.

.... 14. Works effectively with other administrators.

.... 15. ....

.... 16. ....

....   Composite rating.

Form 15.

PERSONNEL
PERFORMANCE APPRAISAL REPORT

A. PURPOSE:

The Performance Appraisal Report covered in this policy is designed to be used in conjunction with the Job Performance and Personal Development Program (Personnel Guide 2.010) *or* completely on its own in order to provide an overall performance review in nine specific areas which are outlined on the form itself.

The Job Performance and Personal Development Program as covered in Personnel Guide 2.010 is geared more toward personnel with managerial responsibilities for whom there can be established specific, measurable goals and objectives. These are usually very quantitative and specific to the particular assignment at hand.

B. PROCEDURE:

1. *Frequency:* New employees should be appraised first no later than three months following their employment date. Subsequent appraisals should be at least each six months for non-exempt employees and at least annually for exempt employees. The specific dates should be determined by the supervisor and should be related perhaps to when a group of specific major duties are completed, after a particular follow-up determined on the last appraisal report, etc. The time periods are felt to be very important because of the need for all employees to have the question answered, "How am I doing?"

2. *Employees Covered:* All salaried (or hourly non-union) exempt and non-exempt employees should be evaluated. For a salaried employee on whom the Job Performance and Personal Development form is completed, the Performance Appraisal Report is a natural summary appraisal that should be used as an adjunct.

The form is equally applicable to hourly employees who have supervisory responsibilities because of the universality of the nine rating areas discussed. It is an excellent developmental tool and also one that is very suited to employees being considered for more responsible positions either within the hourly classifications or within management. For drivers and helpers, the Personnel Performance Review forms are already used as part of the Professional Mover's Program. The Performance Appraisal Report discussed here, however, is still of use for members of these classifications as explained in the above paragraph.

3. *Distribution:* The form should be completed in duplicate, with the original placed in the employee's personnel folder and the copy given to the employee. Local management will want to establish routing procedures.

4. *Guidelines for Appraisal:* It is very easy to let recent incidents and events color our evaluation of employees as opposed to letting our

entire review period truly be what we are evaluating. It is important to let the performance during the entire period be the basis for the review and rating. Isolated or unusual incidents should not color the entire rating.

Personal feelings have no business in an objective rating of performance. Only factors which relate to job performance should be included. For example, it should not be your concern whether an employee wears a blue or yellow shirt even though you might prefer one color over another. The color of the shirt can only matter if it can be directly related to the employee's performance in his job.

There must be specific standards and objectives against which you are rating the employee. Therefore, it is important that, before the beginning of the rating period, you and your employee have a clear understanding as to what you expect from him on the job.

A good technique to use is to have the employee complete the Performance Appraisal Report prior to his performance review as a method of determining his own self-analysis. If an employee points out his own weaknesses, for example, it will give you a basis for discussion in sensitive areas where it might otherwise be difficult to introduce the subject.

Salary reviews are not necessarily to occur at the same time a Performance Report is prepared. Naturally, if an employee has an excellent appraisal review, it means he is doing an excellent job. This should not automatically mean, however, that he is going to be recommended for a raise in salary that same day. Money should not be the only motivator.

5. *Completion of the Form:* The nine factors listed pertain to job-related characteristics which are applicable to every job within the company. Suggestions are given following each factor to help you relate that particular factor to your employee. Several rating descriptions pertaining to each of the nine factors are given, and you are asked to check the rating description which most nearly reflects your objective evaluation of the employee concerning the factor being measured. Room is given for you to substantiate the rating checked in order to qualify and quantify it more specifically as it relates to the employee.

You are asked to complete the following additional items on the form:

a. *Self-Development Activities:* During the interview with the employee, part of the discussion should revolve around what the employee has done or intends to do concerning his own development pertaining to his career, etc.

b. *Overall Effectiveness:* This section should be that rating which, in your judgment, most completely describes the *total* current performance of this employee in relationship to the job requirements you have established.

    c. *Weaknesses of the Employee:* In this section should be stated the job-related weaknesses that, in your opinion, are areas that the employee should devote his efforts in overcoming.

    d. *Strengths of the Employee:* When listing the employee's strengths, these should pertain to the most important characteristics of that employee that make him successful in the job he is in, as well as perhaps make him a good candidate for future advancement.

    e. *Specific Plans to Improve Performance:* This is one of the most important areas on the form. Here is the opportunity for you and the employee at the conclusion of your interview to mutually agree on some specifics to be worked on between then and the next performance review, geared to improving the employee's performance.

C. CONTROL:

1. *Regional/Local:* Each region/location should determine its own methods of ensuring that appraisals are completed in a timely manner on all covered employees.

2. *Corporate:* Inclusion in the personnel folder of a properly completed evaluation form for the correct time period will be part of the audit procedure followed by the Corporate Office audit team.

    Step 4: checkpoints are established for the evaluation of his progress, ways of measuring progress are selected.

    Step 5: the superior and subordinate meet at the end of the period to discuss the results of the subordinate's efforts to meet the targets he had previously established.

    Business and industry, and especially the military, are ahead of higher education in evaluating administrators. While considerable differences exist, we in education can learn from others. The Kindall and Gatza article, for example, in different language nicely outlines the steps of the contract system discussed in higher education; Bekins' "management by objectives" also is worthwhile.

Key Positions

    The list of administrative functions is long and diverse, and varies considerably according to position. The following section touches on evaluative procedures for the president, the academic vice–president, college deans, and department chairmen.

Text continued on Page 96

FORM 16.

PERFORMANCE APPRAISAL REPORT

Date ....

Employee Name ....

Report of Performance:

From .... To ....

Department .... Occupation ....

Time in this Classification:

Years .... Months .... Employment Date ....

INSTRUCTIONS

1. All employees should be appraised at least annually.

2. Use in conjunction with the Job Performance and Personal Development Program, where applicable.

3. Review employee's work performance for the entire period; refrain from basing judgment on recent events or isolated incidents only.

4. Do not allow personal feelings to govern your rating. Disregard your general impression of the employee.

5. Consider the employee on the basis of the standards you expect to be met for the job. Place a check by the area you feel best describes the employee's performance since the last appraisal.

6. *Reason must be given for each factor to substantiate area checked.*

QUALITY OF WORK—Consider standard of workmanship, accuracy, neatness, skill, thoroughness, economy of materials, organization of job.

Fully Meets Job Requirements	Meets Minimum Requirements ....
Unsatisfactory Does Not Meet Minimum Requirements	Exceeds Job Requirements ....
	Other (*Specify*) ....

Reason: ....

....

....

VOLUME OF WORK—Consider use of time, the volume of work accomplished and ability to meet schedules, productivity levels.

Does Not Meet Job Requirements	Meets Minimum Job Requirements ....
Exceeds Job Requirements	Fully Meets Job Requirements ....
	Other (*Specify*) ....

Reason: ....

....

....

PERSONAL WORK HABITS—Consider safety, housekeeping and compliance with company practices, proper dress, appearance, personal hygiene, neatness, cleanliness.

| Very Good .... | Satisfactory .... |
| Improvement Needed ... . | Outstanding .... |

Reason: ....

....

....

ADAPTABILITY—Consider ability to meet changing conditions and situations, ease with which the employee learns new duties and assignments.

| Improvement Needed ... . | Outstanding .... |
| Satisfactory .... | Very Good .... |

Reason: ....

....

....

JUDGMENT—Consider ability to evaluate relative merit of ideas or facts and arrive at sound conclusions, ability to decide correct course of action when some choice can be made.

| Very Good .... | Satisfactory .... |
| Needs Much Improvement .... | Outstanding .... |

Reason: ....

....

....

JOB KNOWLEDGE AND SKILL—Consider understanding of job procedures and methods, ability to acquire necessary skills, expertness, and utilization of background for job.

Fully Meets Job Requirements ....   Meets Minimum Job Requirements ....

Improvement Needed ... .   Exceeds Job Requirements ....

Reason: ....

....

....

ATTITUDE—Consider cooperation with supervisor and co-workers; receptiveness to suggestions and constructive criticisms; attitude toward Company; enthusiasm, attempts to improve performance.

Exceeds Job Requirements ....   Meets Minimum Job Requirements ....

Fully Meets Job Requirements ....   Improvement Needed ... .

Reason: ....

....

....

CUSTOMER RELATIONS—Consider telephone conversations as well as direct personal contact. Does employee deal tactfully with customer? Does employee satisfy their request? Does employee meet our service and courtesy requirements? (*Use where applicable*)

Fully Meets Job Requirements ....   Needs Much Improvement ....

Satisfactory ....   Outstanding ....

Reason: ....

....

....

TEAM EFFORT—LEADERSHIP—Consider ability to inspire teamwork, enthusiasm to work towards a common objective, desire to assume responsibility, ability to originate or develop ideas and to get things started, ability to train others.

Does Not Meet Job Requirements ....   Meets Minimum Job Requirements ....

Exceeds Job Requirements ....   Fully Meets Job Requirements ....

Reason: ....
....
....

SELF-DEVELOPMENT ACTIVITIES—Of this employee (*To be completed during interview*)

....
....

PRESENT STATUS—NEEDS—PLAN OF ACTION

OVERALL EFFECTIVENESS—Considering the amount of experience on present job, check the rating which most nearly describes total current performance.

Exceeds Job
Requirements ....

Fully Meets Job
Requirements ....

Does Not Meet Job
Requirements ....

Meets Minimum Job
Requirements ....

WHAT ASPECTS OF PERFORMANCE—If not improved, might hinder future development or cause difficulty in present classification (Weakness of employee)?

....
....

WHAT ARE GREATEST STRENGTHS OF EMPLOYEE?

....
....

GIVE SPECIFIC PLANS—You and your employee have made to improve performance

....
....

Employee's Signature (*Does not necessarily indicate concurrence*)

Date ....

President. As chief executive officer of the institution, the president is ultimately responsible for its overall excellence or mediocrity. He has no tenure and serves at the pleasure of the controlling board. His success depends mainly on their support, but the support of others is needed also—a president who does not have faculty support, for instance, cannot serve effectively for long. A president is a juggler of constituencies, seeking to keep positive and stable relationships with his basic ones: trustees, alumni, faculty, students, administrators, staff, and influential others. The trick is to keep in good graces with most constituencies most of the time. He is in trouble if too many are critical at any one time. In one sense, survival is a mark of success—in the same way as it was for a French aristocrat during the French Revolution! But survival as evaluative yardstick is not enough, and more definitive procedures are needed. Here are some suggestions:

First, the board of trustees conducts an evaluation on a regular basis—every three or four years—beginning in September and ending by Christmas. This timetable may allow the president to enjoy the holidays a bit more, and in the few cases where a report recommends that the president seek another position, it provides something of a decompression period for all. A special subcommittee of the board may be appointed, or perhaps the executive committee might serve. The board may want to conduct an initial session to develop an overall plan and procedures for presidential evaluation, with the president assisting in developing the procedure. Utmost sensitivity and confidentiality should be exercised throughout.

First, the trustees should request the president to report (1) what he believes to be his major accomplishments, and (2) the extent to which his activities have been consistent with his job description and the goals of the institution. He should have the option of discussing where he has not made as much progress as hoped.

Second, not every faculty member should be expected or requested to evaluate the president. Some official faculty body—an elected committee or an ad hoc one—should be used. Again, the purpose and procedures should be clearly understood. How should faculty members go about this sensitive and difficult task? Informal and quiet inquiry is the preferable procedure. Since the president is not elected and does not maintain his position on the basis of popularity polls, a facultywide survey is not needed or desired. At the appropriate time, the faculty and the trustee committees should meet, with the trustee committee leading the discussion. Also, the trustee committee may want to discuss the matter with other committees or respected members of the faculty. Always confidentiality should be carefully maintained.

Third, administrators and faculty exist because of students —a simple truth that is sometimes lost sight of. Therefore, students should have a voice in presidential evaluation. Here, too, a popularity contest should be avoided in favor of a more informal, quiet approach. The student body president should work with elected student organizations to develop a view of the presidential effectiveness from a student's perspective. And these findings should be reported in a session with the trustee committee.

Both the procedure and the spirit of the report should accentuate the positive ways in which the president might improve. Faculty evaluation designed primarily to gain data for salaries, promotion, and tenure is viewed negatively by faculty members; and the same logic applies to administrative evaluation. Emphasis should be on strengths and on those areas where improvement is desirable. The suggestions should have enough specificity so the president can work on them.

Kingman Brewster, president of Yale University, set forth this position on presidential accountability:

> The principle of executive accountability as the price which must be paid for the exercise of executive discretion has, up to now, been formally limited to the power of the trustees to fire the man they hired as president. . . . There is no objective occasion or event which invites this appraisal. Even the most decorous and covert effort to remove an unsatisfactory president is at best a matter of intense personal anguish to everyone concerned. . . . The essence of the problem is that, while there is legal accountability to the trustees, there is no orderly way in which those most significantly affected by maladministration can invoke trustee action within a measurable time without open challenge to the stability of the institution and the integrity of its process. . . . I think Yale would be better off if it were understood that the trustees would make a

systematic reappraisal and explicit consideration of the President's appointment at some specified interval. This might be seven years after the initial appointment, perhaps at a somewhat shorter interval thereafter.

The Board of Trustees of the State University of New York adopted (1973) a policy requiring presidential evaluation every five years and a professional leave policy for chief administrative officers. In part it states:

Section 333.1 Appointment. (a) There shall be a chief administrative officer of each college. He shall be appointed by the Board of Trustees, after receipt of recommendations of the college council and also of the Chancellor, and shall serve *for a period of five years, during which period the appointee shall serve* at the pleasure of the Board of Trustees. Before making its recommendations the college council shall consult with the committee of the college faculty, designated for such purpose by the faculty and with representatives of the administrative staff and the student body. The Chancellor, or his designated representative, before making his recommendations to the Trustees, shall consult with the chairman or other designated representative of the college council.

(b) *Unless reappointed, the service of a chief administrative officer shall terminate at the conclusion of an appointive period. Prior to the expiration of any appointive period the Board of Trustees may formally evaluate the services of the chief administrative officer and may reappoint the incumbent to serve at the pleasure of the Board for a subsequent five year period.*

Section 337.31 Third Year of Service. Upon recommendation of the Chancellor, the Board of Trustees may grant the chief administrative officer of each college a two month study leave at full salary during every third year of service subsequent to the date of initial appointment of the date of the last leave taken pursuant to this Title, in lieu of vacation leave accrued for the third year of service. Such leave shall be for the specific purpose of improving the administrative and academic performance of the chief administrative officer.

337.32 Five Years of Service. Upon recommendation of the Chancellor, the Board of Trustees may grant the chief administrative officer of each college a one semester study leave at full salary at the end of a period of five years of service in lieu of vacation leave accrued for the year in which the leave is taken. Such leave shall be for the specific purpose of improving the administrative and academic performance of the chief administrative officer . . . .

Academic vice-president. Procedures for evaluating each vice–president are not discussed, although the general pattern would follow that for the academic vice–president. The latter is chosen because of the particularly difficult and sensitive nature of his position.

Depending on the organizational pattern, the academic vice-president reports either to the executive vice–president, provost, or the president, but in any case his evaluation should be the direct responsibility of the president. Inputs should be from three clienteles: the faculty, other administrators, and the president. It is generally unwise to conduct a facultywide survey of the dean's popularity although there always seem to be exceptions. The academic dean of one private liberal arts college in Ohio, of about 1500 students, wrote this account:

Each spring I distribute to all faculty members a questionnaire which I make up each spring. I do this because, as I sense the weak points in my job function, I ask questions related to those weak points. It permits me to find out things about myself and to check on comments that have been made from time to time. I realize the difficulty, of course, in comparing one year to the next, but the overall value of being able to adapt the questionnaire to the needs of the moment seems to outweigh the difficulty of not being able to make year to year comparisons. The questionnaire goes out in May and is returned sometime before the end of the academic year. I then summarize the responses and make an analysis. I then meet with the President to discuss the results of the evaluation and to work on procedures for satisfying whatever complaints seem to be made which indicate some special effort.

As with the president, the academic dean should be asked to submit a statement of what he considers his accomplishments and on how well he has moved toward fulfilling his own job description and the institutional goals.

Normally, the academic dean will be evaluated by representatives of the faculty, deans of the colleges, and by the president. Evaluation by faculty may take place through any of several mechanisms, such as a faculty executive committee or a special committee appointed by the president—the mechanism is not as important as the spirit of the dispassionate and discrete inquiry, with the dean having full opportunity to present views. The final report should be given to the president and to the academic dean. All typing should be done in the president's office and all records maintained by the president, except for the copy to the academic dean.

The academic dean's evaluation by college deans should differ from that conducted by the president and faculty. Since college deans usually are appointed by the academic dean and therefore are in a delicate position, one procedure might be to have one dean serve as a spokesman, conveying to the academic dean the essence of the views expressed by all. Written comments should be typed in the president's office with all other copies destroyed. The reporting procedure might be a conference of the reporting dean, the academic dean, and the president.

In summary, the academic dean's evaluation should be a synthesis of views of the president, the faculty, and other administrators, and should reflect the highest professional standards and the greatest personal sensitivities. But in the final analysis, the president must decide on the overall effectiveness of the academic dean, and the dean should always keep this in mind. Occasionally a dean may seek to play the faculty against the president to strengthen or preserve his own position. Such strategy is likely to boomerang because the president does have the authority to remove him should their working relationship become unproductive.

College deans. College deans have the interests of their academic area and academicians foremost in mind, as pointed out by a former dean of Yale College: "Perhaps the greatest difficulty I have had as dean is in trying to get departments to consider the good of the college as a more important matter than the advancement of the discipline which they represent" (DeVane, 1968, p.

246). Their evaluation should take into consideration the views of department chairmen, certain faculty groups within the college, the academic dean, and perhaps other academic deans. Some universities assist the process by enacting governing procedures which limit deans and department heads to one or two terms. If the procedure calls for thorough evaluation after one five-year term the academic dean and the president have an opportunity to change college deans through institutionalized procedures with perhaps a minimum of disruption. Again, as with the president and the academic dean, the process should include a detailed report by the dean on his accomplishments and institutional contributions.

The academic dean should be directly responsible for the evaluation of the respective college deans. He might approach department chairmen individually with a series of questions, with notetaking for his own records. Also, the academic dean should ask some faculty group within the college for its evaluation. Confidentiality must be stressed. The faculty committee and academic dean should meet, with the academic dean taking notes. Written statements may be used but one must weigh the risk of leaks, probably more at this level than any other. The academic dean, however, should have his notes typed for the files.

The academic dean meets with the respective college deans for an evaluation session, and the evaluative report should be in writing with a copy to the president. In cases of questionable performance, the academic dean might want to include the provost or executive vice-president. And in any case, the college dean should have the right of appeal directly to the president.

Department chairmen. In *The Confidence Crisis* Dressel and others (1970) wrote "the chairman may play the role of honest broker, attempting to interpret accurately to both the department and the dean the concerns and dissatisfactions of the other. He may play one against the other to enhance his own position, in which case his days as chairman may be numbered. Or he may attempt to cater to the dissatisfactions of one, forcing its demands upon the other, in which case the days of his life may be lessened by ulcers, high blood pressure, or heart failure. Only the honest broker role produces healthy reciprocated confidence. Diminishing or no confidence was demonstrated by frequent replacement of the chairman, by high rates of faculty turnover, inadequate support, and decline in quality of the departmental program." Obviously the chairman needs to be evaluated by both faculty members in the department as well as by the college dean. The procedure may take one of many forms, depending on such factors as departmental size, institutional traditions, and governance structure. Whether the entire department, tenured members, or a faculty committee does the evaluating depends on the factors mentioned. In any case, the department chairman should have a face-to-face reporting session with the college dean, and the chairman should have recourse to the academic dean if he so desires.

Many other administrative roles should also be evaluated: the admissions and registrar activities, the computer services, counseling activities. Each needs a somewhat different, even distinct, approach. But to be consistent with the principle of administration these procedures should be developed, tried, and undoubtedly modified to meet discovered weaknesses. The field of administrative evaluation is new but no less important than faculty evaluation.

Institutional Evaluation

Another dimension of evaluation that will become more evident in the years immediately ahead is institutional evaluation. Pace (1972) writes about a concept of evaluation for large and complex institutions; beginning with the central question, "What are the consequences?" rather than with the more limiting one, "What are the objectives." Its style of inquiry is more aptly characterized by the word *exploration* than by the words *control* and *forms;* it sees the evaluator's role as social scientist rather than a reformer or staff officer to the practitioners; and its purpose is to provide more complex bases for informed judgment. Pace contends that *decision-making* is too narrow a focus for describing the purpose and role of evaluation, *explanation* is too abstract and impersonal, leaving *judgment* as the central orientation for evaluation studies of large and complex institutions.

Several instruments for measuring institutional vitality are available, and cost-accounting procedures are becoming commonplace. But we will need to find ways of identifying and developing the *qualitative* measures of institutional vitality. Quantitative data are means to ends—a richer education, and this means-ends relationship needs to be remembered as we move further into the computer age.

Epilogue

After two books on evaluation, first-hand experience (professor, director of studies, department chairman, academic vice-president, state board of higher education official) with faculty evaluation in several types of institutions and many consultations at other institutions, I have developed these general impressions:

To begin with, faculty evaluation must always be kept in perspective. The primary mission of almost every college and university is education of young adults. That simple truth should not be obscured. To accomplish this, colleges and universities employ faculty members to teach and administrators to administer—and many wish the reality was that simple. The majority of faculty members are serious students of their respective disciplines and, within their given circumstances, are doing a professionally sound job. This does not say that improvement is not possible; it is, and faculty evaluation can improve performance by allowing one to see himself as others see him. When the purpose of one's life work is to influence others, it is altogether fitting that the views of others count.

A small minority of faculty members are doing little more than drawing their paychecks. They have psychologically tuned out of the dynamism and excitement of their discipline and may even resent others who have not. These individuals need every encouragement and sympathetic support, and they may also need some less gentle pressures. Someone pays for the salaries of all college and university personnel—either the state or private citizens. In either case, they have the right to insist—and they are increasingly doing so—on positive results. Faculty evaluation can assist the administration and faculty colleagues in discerning which individuals are performing at acceptable levels. This function is not punitive but diagnostic, and if the evaluation is well-conceived and administered properly, it can be one of the fairest ways of making sound decisions about professional performance.

Administrative evaluation is desirable and necessary, and it is not fair nor consistent to advocate faculty evaluation without advocating administrative evaluation, too. And evaluation should not stop with administrators; it should be institutionwide and include support personnel and various administrative roles also. How does one measure institutional quality? Is it by the number of Nobel Prize winners on the faculty, the cost-ratios of degree production, average income of graduates, contributions to professional fields, and so forth? Little is known about these larger questions regarding institutional evaluation.

Some enthusiasts of faculty and administrative evaluation are likely to confuse means with ends. Faculty and administrative evaluation are means to the larger ends of learning, they are not ends in themselves. Further, they are one of several means of professional development and should be directed toward more effective performance. Enthusiasts sometimes ascribe more to faculty evaluation than it should—or could—deliver.

Finally a college or university is a human community—a unique institution in society. Its products and its on-going activities account for most human progress and inventions; its traditions and mores cause frustrations and misunderstandings among its critics; its freedoms provide an essential bulwark for the democratic way of life; and its concern for idealism and ideas has kindled the hopes and dreams of millions who have "found" themselves during college days. Most of them are better people because of this brief period, and this is what counts. Evaluation then is one way of improving the quality of this experience. If done sensitively and intelligently, it can be very constructive.

Selected and Annotated Bibliography

This Bibliography should be of assistance to those interested in research on faculty evaluation, those who have practical operational problems to solve, those considering the development or evaluation of a system of faculty evaluation, and those interested in qualitative dimensions of institutional evaluation.

The entries in the Bibliography are indexed in the general index both by subject and by author. Works cited but not annotated are not evaluation studies.

ABELSON, P. A. "Justifying Academic Research." *Science,* 1967, *157,* 759.

A serious failure of academicians has been in educating the public about the role of scholarly inquiry in the universities. The necessity to do so became acute a few years previously when a number of articles in major publications asserted that research efforts by professors were destructive to the teaching functions of universities. Critics failed to mention that often the most incompetent professors are those who do no research. With science evolving rapidly, a major task for professors is to keep up with developments. To do otherwise defrauds the student in three ways: failure to render proper guidance on recent and frontier subject material and ideas, failure to set high standards of scholarship, and failure to inspire enthusiasm for learning. To be a good teacher of science a professor must be intellectually virile and part of the creative enterprise.

ABRAMSON, P. (Ed.) "Sauce for the Goose Is Sauce for the Gander." *College Management,* 1966, 27–31. (no volume used)

Three out of every ten colleges responding to a 1966 *College Management* survey said they already used some formal system of faculty rating by students or would institute one in the fall. Several systems of student evaluation were surveyed: The University of North Carolina at Chapel Hill, for example, prefers to have graduating seniors evaluate faculty and curriculum. A select group of one hundred seniors—picked from among members of Phi Beta Kappa, high ranking seniors in each of the major disciplines, and student office holders—were asked to make the ratings. Their observations were used to help determine whether the curriculum met student needs, and they also were used as an extra dimension in determining promotions. Every member of the senior class was used at Kalamazoo College in the survey. Each was asked to grade his professors on an overall basis and on certain aspects of their teaching. He was also asked to name his seven best professors in rank order. Answers to this questionnaire were fed into a computer and the results were used primarily to help the teacher but also in tenure and promotions deliberations.

AMERICAN ACADEMY OF ARTS AND SCIENCES. *Assembly on University Goals and Governance: A First Report.* Cambridge, Mass.: The Assembly, 1971.

One thesis of the Report deals with student participation in faculty appraisal, stating: "More systematic appraisal methods need to be introduced to identify and reward successful teachers. Student opinion in these matters is crucial, even though decisions on appointment ought to continue to rest with faculty and administration. Those who secure the benefits of good teaching—the students—ought to be included among the principal guardians of the teaching function. The hazard that such guardianship will encourage and favor showmanship and a quest for popularity can be overcome by policies that balance student preferences with the judgments of others, including colleagues. These judgments should include an estimate of the individual's capacity to attract able students, however few, and the importance of preserving specific fields whether or not they attract students." On the issue of teaching and/or research, the Assembly developed this statement: "The argument has been frequently made that research interests divert professors from their teaching obligations, thereby leading to a neglect of students. This may indeed happen. It is particularly unfortunate when it happens for research or writing that is trivial, motivated largely by pressures for promotion. The challenge, clearly, is to remedy such abuses. To adopt policies that will destroy the vital links between research exploration and imaginative teaching is no remedy. Any attempt to develop a teaching ethic in higher education that would banish research would risk making teaching sterile. The professors who are inclined to do research should be encouraged to do so. This, however, need not mean that the university would welcome every kind of research effort."

ANDERSON, C. C., AND HUNKA, S. M. "Teacher Evaluation: Some Problems and a Proposal." *Harvard Educational Review,* 1963, *33,* 74–95.

Pupils, evaluators, and administrators consider quite different attributes in conceptualizing the competent teacher. A step toward better understanding of the problems relating to teacher competency may be the intensive and extensive study of teacher characteristics. Some of these may be spontaneity, initiative, voluntary social contributions, and acts of problem solving, as contrasted with interpersonal conflict and boredom.

ANDERSON, R. C., AND OTHERS. *Current Research on Instruction.* Englewood Cliffs, N.J.: Prentice-Hall, 1969.

Here is a text or supplementary source for students of education and students of psychology concerned with its application to education. Its main themes are: approaches to instructional research and development, instructional objectives, prompting and fading techniques, the student response, reinforcement and feedback, facilitation of concept learning, organization and sequence, and evaluation of instruction. The articles in sections devoted to the above themes are taken from a variety of sources.

ANIKEEFF, A. M. "Factors Affecting Student Evaluation of College Faculty Members." *Journal of Applied Psychology,* 1953, *37,* 458–460.

The purpose of the study, conducted in the School of Business and Industry at Mississippi State College, was to determine the effect of grading leniency upon student ratings of faculty members. Student absence patterns also were studied. This sampling of approximately 1,500 cases determined that the grades which faculty members assigned students were reflected in the ratings. The extent to which class grades influence students evaluations of faculty members varies with the academic levels of the students. Grading leniency accounts for almost three times as much variance in student rating of faculty on the freshman and sophomore level as it does on the upper levels where the relationship is not statistically significant. Class absences are negatively correlated with faculty ratings.

ASTIN, A. W., AND LEE, C. B. T. "Current Practices in the Evaluation and Training of College Teachers." *The Educational Record,* 1966, *47,* 361–365.

A survey of 1110 institutions was intended to provide an empirical basis for a critical appraisal of the current practices and to determine a point of departure from which proposals for improving existing techniques could be developed.

The most frequently used of fifteen sources of information for determining teacher effectiveness were: evaluations by department chairman (85 percent responded use in all or most departments); evaluations by the dean (82 percent); the opinions of colleagues (49 percent); scholarly research and publications (44 percent); and informal student opinions (41 percent). Classroom visits were used very infrequently (taboo at 40 percent of the institutions); thus evaluations must be based on hearsay evidence (informal student opinions). The data clearly indicate that research and publication are the primary considerations in evaluating teaching ability.

Criteria considered by all institutions as major factors for salary increase, promotion, and tenure were: classroom teaching (96 percent); personal attributes (57 percent); length of service in rank (47 percent); research (47 percent). At universities, research is almost equal in consideration to teaching. More selective and affluent colleges and larger institutions are more likely to use research and publication as criteria.

BACON, F. *Essays,* London: Dent, 1906.

BARR, A. S. "The Appraisal of Teaching in Large Universities: A Summary of Remarks." In W. J. McKeachie (Ed.), *The Appraisal of Teaching in Large Universities.* Ann Arbor, Mich.: The University of Michigan Extension Service, 1959.

Five general observations about the measurement and evaluation of learning and teaching outcomes are given: it is difficult to secure competent observers and evaluators; judgments about teaching should be based upon verifiable evidence and not upon preconceived opinions, sporadic visits, and hearsay evidence; the acts of teachers and pupils must be considered in context; judges need to be trained; and the safest approach to the appraisal of teaching is a multiple one employing more than one theoretical orientation, a variety of data gathering devices, and a number of persons studying teachers and teaching under a variety of conditions.

BAYLEY, D. H. "Making College Teaching a Profession." *Improving College and University Teaching,* 1967, *15,* 115–19.

Although most college teachers believe that they are fully capable of criticizing their own teaching performance, the present system indicates that such evaluations can hardly be accepted at face value. The author sees two alternatives—students and other observers. Since, by and large, teachers reject student evaluations, their worth may be judged by setting them alongside qualified observers—other college teachers. Colleague evaluation will provide trustworthy criticism, an essential element of feedback—agreement as to teaching performance—and information for rewarding and punishing teachers.

BEKINS MOVING AND STORAGE COMPANY. *Performance and Development.* 1970.

BELKNAP, E. H., AND OTHERS. "Guidelines for Promotion." *Improving College and University Teaching,* 1965, *13,* 14–15.

This article discusses recommendations by the Division of Education Personnel Committee at San Fernando State College on policies to be followed in relation to hiring, orientation, and promotion of staff members. They were based on the assumption that faculty promotions are made on the basis of personal judgments. These judgments, then, must be distilled from the largest source of information available to the judges. Information sources were grouped into three areas: good teaching at the college level, contribution to division and college, and professional growth.

BENDIG, A. W. "A Factor Analysis of Student Ratings of Psychology Instructors on the Purdue Scale." *Journal of Educational Psychology,* 1954, *45,* 385–393.

The purpose of this study was to find whether factor analytic techniques applied to student ratings on the Purdue Rating Scale for Instruction (PRSI)' could provide an empirical method of combining separate scales to yield a smaller number of reliable and independent measures of instructor effectiveness. The mean ratings of eleven introductory psychology instructors on the first ten scales of the PRSI were intercorrelated and the resulting matrix was analyzed by a centroid method. Three factors accounted for 80 percent of the variance: a general factor permeating the scales and two group factors that were labelled "instructional competence" and "instructor empathy."

BENDIG, A. W. "The Relation of Level of Course Achievement To Students' Instructor and Course Ratings in Introductory Psychology." *Educational and Psychological Measurement,* 1953, *13,* 437–448.

This research study included 132 students at the University of Pittsburgh, and four items of data were collected: the instructor, standard scores on three achievement examinations given in the previous course, ratings of instructor on first ten items of the Purdue Rating Scale, and sum of course ratings on the other thirteen items of the PRSI. While the rating scales used still demonstrated significant differences in students' evaluation of the course when the factor of known student achievement was statistically controlled, the student achievement test variable was significantly related to the course rating variable. Student achievement was not significantly related to instructor ratings. The author does not reject achievement as a determinant in student rating, but the controlling of the individual student achievement level does not affect the rank order of the instructors. Student achievement does affect the ratings but not to a degree that invalidates the continued use of the scales.

BENDIG, A. W. "Student Achievement in Introductory Psychology and Student Ratings of the Competence and Empathy of their Instructors." *Journal of Psychology,* 1953, *36,* 427–33.

The ratings of 121 sophomore students of five introductory psychology instructors were used to estimate the instructional competence and empathy of the instructors. Analyses of variance indicated significant differences between instructors on both traits, no overall difference between men and women student ratings for either trait but a significant interaction between instructors and students for the trait of competence. Covariance analysis showed a high negative correlation between mean student achievement and mean ratings of instructional competence, but none of the other rating variables were significantly related to student achievement.

BENDIG, A. W. "An Inverted Factor Analysis Study of Student-Rated Introductory Psychology Instructors." *Journal of Experimental Education,* 1953, *21,* 333–336.

The student rating scale profiles of ten introductory psychology instructors were correlated, and the matrix of intercorrelations was factor analyzed by inverted factor techniques. Three factors were extracted—concerning presentation of material, organization of material, and fairness and appearance—two of which were rotated to maximize clustering of instructors into groups. The factor loadings of the instructors were correlated with their scores on each of the fourteen rating scales and the three scales correlating highest with each scale used to describe the extremes of each linear factor. Validity of the factor descriptions was determined by correlating the factor loadings of the instructors with the rankings of the instructors on the three factors by four competent judges. The median validity was .49.

BENDIG, A. W. "A Preliminary Study of the Effect of Academic Level, Sex, and Course Variables on Student Rating of Psychology Instructors." *Journal of Psychology,* 1952, *34,* 21–26.

Sixty-seven students in three different classes of introductory and social psychology courses rated two different instructors on a revised version of the Miami University Instructor Rating Sheet. The main variables of sex, academic level, differences between rating scales, and differences between the instructors were found to affect the ratings significantly. In addition, the instructor teaching both introductory and social psychology was rated differently by his students in the two courses, with these conclusions: female students were more unfavorable than were males in their ratings, and juniors and seniors were more unfavorable than were freshmen and sophomores.

BENDIG, A. W. "The Use of Student-Rating Scales in the Evaluation of Instructors in Introductory Psychology." *Journal of Educational Psychology,* 1952, *43,* 167–175.

The Miami University Instructor Rating Sheet was given anonymously to 617 undergraduate students in introductory psychology. Twelve of the fourteen scales reliably discriminated among the ten daytime instructors at the .001 level and the other two scales at the .09 level. It was concluded that the scales are useful as part of a multiple criterion of teaching effectiveness and can be improved by revision to achieve a more symmetrical distribution of student ratings.

BIRNBAUM, R. "Background and Evaluation of Faculty in New York." *The Junior College Journal,* 1966, *38,* 34–37.

Twelve factors as criteria for promotion and tenure were surveyed at 27 of the 34 public, two-year colleges in New York State. The two top-ranked factors were teaching performance and effectiveness, and academic preparation and continuing education. Last-ranked factors were community service, and scholarly research and publications, respectively. With respect to methods of evaluating teaching effectiveness, the factors ranked one and two involved ratings by administrators.

BLACKMAN, A. F., AND OTHERS. "Students Rate Their Professors and Courses." *Phi Delta Kappan,* 1967, *48,* 266–269.

A booklet in which professors and students would discuss their courses was developed by the authors. Student opinion was solicited by questionnaire, and a summary of the course was written. The professor was then forwarded the summary and invited to reply. His reply was printed along with the summary of the course. The objectives were: to inform students about their prospective courses; to provide professors with feedback about their teaching; and to influence academic policy or effect changes in the teaching of courses. Eighty percent of professors replied to the summaries. A 30 percent student response was needed for a summary to be written.

BLUM, M. L. "An Investigation of the Relation Existing Between Students' Grades and Their Ratings of the Instructor's Ability to Teach." *Journal of Educational Psychology,* 1936, *27,* 217–221.

Are students influenced by their standing in the course in rating instructors? This question was researched in two classes during a summer session at College of the City of New York. The study concludes that the students' actual or estimated course standing does not influence the teaching evaluation. Regardless of whether a student receives an A, B, C, or D in a course, the estimation of the instructor's ability remains essentially the same and closely resembles the average estimation of the total group.

BOGARDUS, E. S. (Ed.) "Behavior Patterns of College Teachers." *Sociology and Social Research,* 1964, *30,* 484–490.

Based upon the author's observations over a nineteen-year period, the following *undesirable* traits of a college teacher are identified: nervous reactions, speech pecularities, careless personal habits, careless professional habits such as tardiness, self-centeredness, inconsiderateness, and excessive moralizing.

BOGUE, E. G. "Student Appraisal of Teaching Effectiveness in Higher Education; Summary of the Literature." *Educational Quest,* 1967, *11,* 6–10.

The article presents various opinions on the need for utilization of student opinions in the evaluative process, for there has been a lack of scientific basis for the educational practice of evaluation. Evaluation does not eliminate the need for value judgment.

BORGATTA, E. F. "Student Rating of Faculty." (A response to the McKeachie article in the December 1969 AAUP *Bulletin*), *AAUP Bulletin,* 1970, *56,* 6–7.

The author notes that student rating procedures may be useful in helping to learn whether a teacher is negligent but they should not be used as evidence in making judgments about comparative effectiveness, promotion, tenure, salaries, or other matters. Some professors may feel that colleges and universities should be thought of as institutions of higher *learning.* Thus one might very well say that it should be emphasized that students are there to learn, *not to be taught.* The author poses the question, What does it mean to be taught? And, if the institutions are for *learning,* then it is of concern to emphasize having learned people on the faculty, with the most revelant criteria concerned with a person's scholarship and contribution to the basis of knowledge at the institution. With such criteria, the relevance of student ratings pales.

BOURGEOIS, D. P. "A Study of Faculty Opinion Concerning Selected Factors Related to Excellence in Teaching at the University of Southwestern Louisiana." Unpublished M. A. thesis. University of Southwestern Louisiana, Lafayette, La., 1967.

A project was undertaken to solicit faculty opinion as to undergraduate program accreditation, benefits derived from educational courses that deal with teacher preparation, promotion policy, and views of the faculty concerning student evaluation. An examination of the literature pertaining to the study indicates that: (1) the Ph.D. does not indicate that a good teacher is produced; (2) the Ph.D. prepares the recipient as a researcher and not as a teacher; (3) only one-half of all who earn a doctorate find their way into teaching; (4) the present graduate colleges train researchers and not teachers; (5) only 10 percent of the faculty accounts for

90 percent of the research and publication in any university; and (6) in any given year, no more than 30 percent of an average university faculty will be engaged in research.

Analysis of questionnaires indicated a lack of qualified faculty members if the proper credential for college teaching is the doctorate. A small percentage of the faculty members had the prescribed professional educational courses required for good college teaching. Many statements also indicated that the faculty was unfamiliar with the policy for promotions at the university. The faculty perceived the students as having some ability to evaluate excellence in teaching, and some benefits could accrue from observation of such a practice.

BOUSFIELD, W. A. "Students' Ratings of Qualities Considered Desirable in College Professors." *School and Society,* 1940, *51,* 253–256.

Sixty-one undergraduates at the University of Connecticut were asked to list in order of importance the five qualities which they regarded as most desirable in a college professor. The ten most desirable qualities, in order of importance, were found to be: fairness, mastery of subject, interesting presentation of material, well-organized material, clearness of exposition, interest in students, helpfulness, ability to direct discussion, sincerity, and keenness of intellect.

BRESLER, J. B. "Teaching Effectiveness and Government Awards." *Science,* 1968, *160,* 164–167.

The study focused on the question, Is the faculty member who publishes and who holds or has held a government award an effective teacher? Three bodies of available data at Tufts University were used in determining where there are meaningful relationships between teaching effectiveness, publication, and the receipt of government support. A search of the literature showed that virtually all comments in the popular literature and most references in professional journals suggest that publication and receipt of support for research somehow detract from teaching performance in the classroom. However, the empirical data of the Tufts study do not support these previous conclusions. The students rated as their best instructors those faculty members who had published articles and who had received or were receiving government support for research.

BREWSTER, K. *Thoughts on University Government.* New Haven, Conn.: The President's Office, Yale University, 1969.

BRICKMAN, W. W. "Student Evaluation of Professors." *School and Society,* 1966, *94,* 143–144.

Reports have indicated the rapid spread of a drive among college students all over the country to evaluate their professors with respect to knowledge of subject matter, teaching effectiveness, and personality. It is questionable, however, if the totality of the student body has the knowledge, experience, and ability to evaluate the professor with a proper degree of accuracy and fairness. That selective student opinion may be helpful may be taken as an axiom, according to the author. However, administrators and faculty should alert themselves to the necessity of devising a system of careful, periodic, objective evaluation of each faculty member's capabilities, performance, and promise in the realms of scholarship, teaching ability, skill in guidance of students, and in other requisite qualities in higher education.

BROUDY, H. S. "Can We Define Good Teaching?" *The Teachers College Record,* 1969, *70,* 583–592.

The author states that good teaching can be defined well enough for experts to use it in instructor evaluation, but chances of reaching agreement are far greater in didactic than in encounter teaching. The machine is the norm for didactic efficiency; the humanely cultivated person is the model for the latter. However, there is an endless variation of the latter model, and the problem for the schools is to lure enough teachers to do the necessary encounter teaching, a task that is more important than defining our preferred variety of it.

BROWN, D. W. "Teach Or Perish." *Improving College and University Teaching,* 1967, *15,* 108–110.

Teaching evaluation requires "five C's." It should be cooperative, comprehensive, constructive, clinical, and continuous. Colleague evaluation should constitute 60 to 75 percent of the final decision. A realistic system of rewards must be provided. Competent analytical study should determine that judgment and evaluation should be thorough and continuous.

BRYAN, R. C. "Student Rating of Teachers." *Improving College and University Teaching,* 1968, *16,* 200–202.

The results of a 1966–1967 survey are summarized. It investigated student-initiated appraisal of teaching. Of the 307 institutions that reported, 149 (49 percent) had a plan for student appraisal of teaching; 117 (38 percent) had never systematically obtained student ratings of teachers; and forty-one (13 percent) had discontinued student ratings after a trial period. Other follow-up questions were sent to the responding institutions.

BRYAN, R. C. "The Teacher's Image Is Stubbornly Stable." *Clearing House,* 1966, *40,* 459–461.

Two studies are reported. One addressed itself to the question, Do high school seniors and college sophomores differ in their opinions of the same teachers? High school seniors were asked to rate forty teachers, then two years later, those who were sophomores in college were asked to react again to the same teachers, using the same opinion questionnaire. The author found that on any given question the number of teachers who made a significant gain ranged from none to two, and the number who made a significant loss ranged from none to two. The second study addressed this question, Can a teacher bring about improvements in the image held by students? The study provided two full years to bring about improvements. It was found that 57 percent of the group that had the benefit of student reaction reports made statistically significant gains on one or more questions, as compared with 24 percent of a control group who did not have student reactions. It should be noted that 43 percent of the teachers failed in the two-year period to show significant gain. These studies indicate that a teacher's image has much stability.

BRYANT, P. T. "By Their Fruits Ye Shall Know Them." *The Journal of Higher Education*, 1967, *38*, 326–330.

Effective teaching, not research, should head the list of considerations for rewards, university administrators agree, according to this report. Three methods for recognizing and rewarding good teaching are discussed. Student evaluation is considered invalid by the author due to student immaturity, elective versus required courses, and class size. Administrative evaluation could be worthwhile; yet it is seldom conducted. Peer evaluation is best conducted by a department chairman or his delegate through visitation, discussion, and examination of course materials and examinations.

BURTON, C. E. *College Teaching*. New York: Harcourt Brace Jovanovich 1956.

Students are in a better position than are teachers or administrators to judge the quality of instruction that they are receiving. The author refers to Aristotle, who mentions in *Politics* that we get a better notion of the merits of the dinner from the guests than from the cook. The prime requirement is that the instructor himself be willing and able to face up to what his students think of his work. Regardless of what verbal defenses college teachers may have, very few can really be indifferent to what their students think. If their defenses are not raised by having a rating system forced on them or by knowledge that the ratings, whatever the subtleties or intricacies of their interpretation, are going to be handled blindly, statistically, and administratively, they are likely to accept student ratings as a source of personal evaluation and guidance. The beginning instructor tends to be so busy with his thoughts and sentences that he often does not have enough time to observe himself in the classroom; yet if he is to be adaptive to the teaching milieu he should be influenced by student reaction. Rating devices make this possible if the instructor can feel that he has control over how the ratings are taken and then interpreted.

BUXTON, C. E. "The Pros and Cons of Training for College Teachers of Psychology." *The American Psychologist*, 1949, *4*, 414–417.

Based upon a survey of twenty-nine departments of Psychology, the author concluded that only a minority of departments were providing much regularized assistance to prospective teacher Ph.D.'s, although the great majority were nevertheless using them as teachers in one capacity or another. He recommends some teacher training prior to the Ph.D., with improvement of teaching as the objective. Making it possible for teaching to be more rewarding in the beginning by making it more skillful is important also. And for those who judge a man not by his teaching but by his research, the first teaching position should be efficient in terms of time and energy to leave some energy for research.

BYRNES, F. C., AND JAMRICH, J. X. "Survey of Policies and Practices Relating to Improved Instruction." *Improvement of Instruction in Higher Education*. Report to The American Association of Colleges for Teacher Education, Washington, D.C., 1962.

Policies and practices relating to instruction were surveyed. Analysis of the 310 questionnaires returned from member institutions indicates that promotion and salary increases are the two reward practices most frequently mentioned. Outstanding teaching alone serves as a basis for promotion in rank in 52 percent of the institutions, while 87 percent indicate salary increases are made on this basis. The appraisal and evaluation technique used by 63 percent in assessing teaching ability for promotion or salary increases is information gathered via the grapevine. Administration observance is reported by 46 percent, with this being least characteristic of universities with enrollments exceeding 25,000. Eighty-eight percent, however, indicate that the administrators evaluate teaching for purposes of salary increases and promotion. Peer group appraisal, student achievement, and student rating systems are also discussed.

CENTRA, J. A. *The Relationship Between Student and Alumni Ratings of Teachers.* Princeton, N.J.: Educational Testing Service, 1973.

A survey revealed that student and alumni ratings for twenty-three teachers were found to correlate .75 and somewhat less for teachers rated only by graduates of their department. This substantial agreement between current students and alumni (of five years) regarding effective or ineffective teachers suggests that student ratings are fairly permanent and do, at least in part, reflect overall, long-term effects of instruction.

CENTRA, J. A. Unpublished letter to *Science,* October 17, 1972.

"Rodin and Rodin (Sept. 29, 1972) conclude that student evaluations of teaching are not valid measures of effective teaching because their ratings were negatively correlated (−.75) with 'amount learned by the students.' It seems to me that an alternative explanation of the findings is equally defensible.

Their sample consisted of only twelve sections taught by teaching assistants. These teaching assistants met with their classes two of the five days (the professor lectured on the other three), answering questions about the lectures and homework on one day and administering or going over test problems in calculus on the second day. The teaching assistants, then, were not teaching the course in the traditional sense (that is, they did not organize the course, choose assignments, and so forth) but mainly were helping those students *who needed help*. This leads us to the criterion that the Rodins used: the number of problems done correctly by students by the end of the quarter. Isn't it likely that the students who had little need of help in doing the calculus problems would not only obtain the best grades but also rate the teaching assistant lowest in total teaching performance? And at the same time, wouldn't there be a tendency for those who rated their teaching assistant highest to be not only students most in need of help but also those who ended up solving the fewest number of problems? In other words, aid provided by the teaching assistant—their teaching performance—may have had little to do with the number of problems that students completed.

It is unfortunate that the Rodins did not provide the correlations for the subquestions included in their teacher ratings scale; those correlations may have provided additional clues to help interpret the findings. It also would have been helpful to have had student ratings of the lecturer-professor.

Although the authors criticized two fairly old validity studies, other recent studies have reported moderate relationships between objective measures of student learning and students' ratings of various dimensions of teaching. In view of the many factors that determine how much students learn in a course, not the least of which is their own motivation and interest, it's probably not reasonable to expect more than the moderate correlations usually reported in these types of validity studies."

CENTRA, J. A. "Self-Ratings of College Teachers: A Comparison with Student Ratings." In J. A. Centra, *The Utility of Student Ratings for Instructional Improvement*. Princeton, N.J.: Educational Testing Service, 1972.

The purpose of this study was to further investigate college teachers' self-ratings and ratings given by students by comparing them over a wide range of specific, student-oriented instructional practices. Discrepancies between self-ratings (or self-descriptions) and those provided by students would underscore the need for student feedback to the instructor as well as highlight specific areas of instruction where feedback is most essential. A comparison of the two types of ratings in over three hundred classes at five colleges disclosed a modest relationship between the two sets of evaluations. The median correlation for seventeen items was .21, indicating that faculty members generally evaluate or describe their teaching somewhat differently from the way it is evaluated or described by their students. The highest correlations occurred for the more factual items on which there was less chance for disagreement, while items eliciting opinions resulted in the lowest correlations. Comparisons between student and faculty responses were also made across items, and a rank correlation of .77 indicated much similarity in the way the two groups ranked the items. There were differential discrepancies noted for various subject areas: teachers of natural science subjects underestimated (relative to their students) both the pace of their course and their students' efforts, while teachers of education and applied subjects overestimated the course pace and their students' efforts.

CENTRA, J. A. "The Effectiveness of Student Feedback in Modifying College Instruction." In J. A. Centra, *The Utility of Student Ratings for Instructional Improvement*. Princeton, N.J.: Educational Testing Service, 1972.

The purpose of this study was to investigate the effects of feedback from student ratings on changing instructional practices at the college level. Teachers within each of five diverse colleges were assigned randomly to a feedback (treatment), no-feedback (control), or post-test group, and over four hundred teachers and their students participated in the study. Some findings were: students perceived natural science teachers as less open to other viewpoints; humanities teachers were less likely to inform students of how they were to be evaluated, and there was less agreement between announced objectives and what was actually taught; women teachers were more likely to know when students did not know the material, were more concerned with student progress, made more comments on papers or examinations, and generally made better use of class time. Courses taught by male teachers were more stimulating and more difficult. The more experienced teachers were rated no better than were those in their first or second years of teaching; in fact, on informing students of how they would be evaluated in the course, the more experienced teachers were rated less favorably. If student feedback improved instruction, end-of-semester ratings of the feedback group should have been better than either the no-feedback or the post-test groups. Multivariate analysis of variance results for the end-of-semester ratings, however, indicated no significant differences among the three groups. Furthermore, no differences were noted when various interactions were investigated. A major hypothesis of this study was that student feedback would effect changes in teachers who had rated themselves more favorably than did their students. Results of the regression analyses indicated this to be the case; the findings suggested that the greater the discrepancy—where the discrepancy reflected the extent to which students rated teachers less favorably than the teachers apparently expected—the greater the likelihood of change.

CHEIT, E. F. *Coming of Middle Age in Higher Education.* Address to the National Association of State Universities and Land-Grant Colleges and American Association of State Colleges and Universities. Washington, D.C., Nov. 13, 1972.

CLARK, K. E., AND KELLER, R. J. "Student Ratings of College Teaching." In R. E. Eckert and R. J. Keller (Eds.), *A University Looks at Its Program.* Minneapolis: University of Minnesota Press, 1954.

The University of Minnesota obtained 14,916 student ratings in 1949, from an instrument developed there. An analysis of the data revealed these findings: there were practically no differences between ratings given by brighter students and those with poorer grades, although students whose average grades were below C assigned their instructors a higher mean rating in general teaching ability than did students reporting average grades higher than C. Professors and associate professors maintained consistently higher averages on general teaching ability and the majority of the other twenty items than did those of lower rank. Those teaching in humanities and natural sciences were more favorably regarded than were those in the social studies on general teaching ability and most of the other twenty items. Seniors and graduate students were much more favorable than were lower classmen. On class size: the least rapport was found in classes of intermediate size, between forty and two hundred students. On the hour of the class: classes held during the middle of the day tended to receive higher mean ratings than did early morning classes which, in turn, were regarded more favorably than were those held in late afternoon.

CLARK, S. J., AND MILLER, P. L. "Student Evaluation of Teachers—Is It Useful, Consistent, and Honest?" Speech, Annual Meeting of the American Society for Engineering Education, June 22, 1971, Annapolis, Md.

After six consecutive semesters of teacher evaluation in the College of Engineering at Kansas State University, an effort was made to determine whether student evaluation of teachers is useful, honest, and consistent. To obtain teacher and student input, questionnaires were sent to a sample of engineering students and teachers. Both groups generally considered teacher evaluation to be useful and honest. Teachers liked the feedback, although they expressed some concern over whether the true-false questions that were used were appropriate for a teaching situation. (Other types of questions were used also.) Students appreciated the opportunity to rate teachers, although a few believed that teachers would not change as a result of their evaluation.

Of the 150 teachers evaluated, seventy-one received ratings in the upper one-third, and fourteen were in the upper one-third every time.

CLINTON, R. J. "Qualities College Students Desire in College Instructors." *School and Society,* 1930, *32,* 702.

The writer asked 177 college students in their junior year at Oregon State University what qualities they desired in their college teachers. The students were left free to write whatever they wished. The ten most frequently listed qualities were: a thorough knowledge of the subject matter (96), a pleasing personality (73), neatness in appearance and in work (57), fairness to all students (50), kind and sympathetic with all students (46), a keen sense of humor (43), an interest in the profession (41), an interesting presentation of subject matter (41), an alertness and broad-mindedness (36), and a knowledge of methods (34).

COFFMAN, W. E. "Determining Students' Concepts of Effective Teaching from Their Ratings of Instructors." *Journal of Educational Psychology,* 1954, *45,* 277–286.

The study included fifty-nine teachers and approximately two thousand students at Oklahoma A and M and used a rating scale developed there. The four reference factors extracted by the central centroid method, and rated highest by the students, were: empathy; organization; the punctual, neat, "normal" individual; and verbal fluency. The general conclusion is that students are competent assessors of teaching. The items of understanding the learner, classroom organization, and verbal fluency are significant aspects of teaching that can be judged effectively by students.

COHEN, A. M., AND BRAWER, F. B. *Measuring Faculty Performance.* Washington, D.C.: American Association of Junior Colleges, 1969, and ERIC Clearinghouse for Junior College Information, University of California at Los Angeles, Number ED031222.

This report is based upon two major theses: (1) teaching performance as a criterion can be established by such media as supervisor ratings, tests, self- and peer evaluations, and observational techniques; and (2) teaching performance must itself be evaluated ultimately in terms of effectiveness. The only valid and stable measure of effectiveness is pupil change—simultaneously, the end product and the single, operationally measurable kind of criterion that can describe teaching effectiveness. Chapters are: the media of faculty measurement, evaluation through personality variables, ratings of college teaching interns, a critique of current practices, the ultimate criterion, and student gain and instructional supervision. A bibliography is included.

COHEN, S. "Evaluation of Teachers." *Journal of Dental Education,* 1967, *30,* 225–228.

Teachers are presently evaluated for two main purposes— recruitment and promotion. Recruitment factors usually have little bearing on teaching competence, and promotion often depends upon how well the candidate is liked. Deans and department heads are generally responsible for evaluation. Priority has been placed on the ability to do research. Suggestions for additional study may include classifying teachers into categories such as seminar leader, lecturer-teacher, clinical teacher, laboratory teacher, and so forth. Benefits of objective teacher evaluation include teacher recognition, enhancement of student learning, and security for teacher and student.

COLLIVER, J. A. "A Report on Student Evaluation of Faculty Teaching Performance at Sangamon State University." *Technical Paper No. 1.* Springfield, Ill.: Division of Academic Affairs, 1972.

Salary and promotion decisions were made on a merit basis at Sangamon State University for the 1971–1972 academic year. Decisions were based on a teaching rating and a service rating. The teaching factor was determined by student ratings of the seventy-five faculty members on a questionnaire which was administered to all classes during that academic year. Additional analyses resulted in these findings: no relationship was found between class size and evaluation or between whether the class was a lecture or a discussion-type course. The number of times a course had been taught by a faculty member was unrelated to evaluation; and academic rank, salary, experience, and highest degree held also were unrelated to evaluation. Students who did not sign the evaluation forms gave significantly lower evaluations than did students who signed the forms. Also, there was no relation between the grade that a student received in class and the evaluation the student gave the faculty member.

COMAFORD, C. "Changes in Student Rating of Instructors." Quoted in R. E. Eckert and R. J. Keller. "Student Ratings of College Teaching." In *A University Looks at Its Program.* Minneapolis: The University of Minnesota Press, 1954.

What happens to student ratings when they are repeated in the same or different courses over a period of time? Twenty-eight instructors at the University of Minnesota were rated one or two quarters apart between spring 1950 and winter 1951. Ten of them were rerated in the same course while the balance were rerated in different courses. The 5 percent level (T-test) was considered significant. The significant mean increases (item gains) greatly exceeded the significant mean decreases (item losses), the ratio being four to one for the same course and two to one for different courses. A nineteen to one ratio of increases to decreases was found on "How would you rate your instructor in general (all-around) teaching ability?" The author speculates that those instructors who repeated the rating scale have improved in teaching ability from one quarter to another and that this improvement may be partially due to the reaction of the instructor to the earlier rating.

COOK, J. M., AND NEVILLE, R. F. *The Faculty as Teachers: A Perspective on Evaluation,* Report 13. Washington, D.C.:

ERIC Clearinghouse on Higher Education, One Dupont Circle, 1971.

This report reviews current evaluation methods, and makes a recommendation for the implementation of an approach. Teaching effectiveness is defined as the study of teaching outcomes. The authors analyze the relative merits of measurement based on student performance (direct measurement) and measurement based on teaching activities (indirect measurement).

CORTEZ, J. D. *The Design and Validation of an Evaluative Instrument to Appraise the Teaching Effectiveness of the College Instructor.* Doctoral dissertation. University of Denver, 1967. (Dissertation Abstracts, Vol. 28, Number 2435-A, 1967).

A three-phase study examined: the design of the evaluative instrument, the evaluative procedure to test its operational feasibility, and the implementation of the evaluative procedure in seven colleges and universities in Colorado. It concludes that the Professional Competence Guide is a practical instrument for evaluating teaching effectiveness and professional competence.

COSGROVE, D. J. "Diagnostic Rating of Teacher Performance." *Journal of Educational Psychology,* 1959, *50,* 200–204.

The article outlines a method for evaluating teaching. The method is a modification of the forced-choice technique, and it may be used to develop diagnostic profiles for alerting the teacher to what students consider to be his strong and weak points. Based upon an initial descriptive check list of nine hundred phrases and reduced to 190 through expert opinion, five final categories were developed with student assistance: mastery and organization of subject matter; skill in the control and discipline of students; reasonableness of demands on student time and effort in view of help and directions given; efficiency and logicality of classroom management procedure; and skill in motivating, inspiring, and creating confidence in students. The profile indicates the teacher's standing on the categories relative to one another and not to any external standard.

COSTIN, F., AND OTHERS. "Student Ratings of College Teaching: Reliability, Validity, and Usefulness." *Review of Educational Research,* 1971, *41,* 511–535.

This article reviews extensively and critically empirical findings concerned with the reliability, validity, and usefulness of student ratings. It is recommended as the most complete and useful summary to date. Its review of empirical studies indicates that students' ratings can provide reliable and valid information on the quality of courses and instruction. Such information can be of use to academic departments in constructing normative data for the evaluation of teaching and may aid the individual instructor in improving his teaching effectiveness. The authors emphasize that student ratings fall far short of a complete assessment of an instructor's teaching contribution. Other factors should be taken into account in any overall measure of instruction.

CRANNELL, C. W. "A Preliminary Attempt to Identify the Factors in Student-Instructor Evaluation." *The Journal of Psychology,* 1953, *36,* 417–422.

An analysis of an experimental rating sheet containing twenty-one items, administered in several different classes to three hundred students, led to the tentative identification of three clusters of components or factors involved in student appraisal of their instructors. These clusters have been named "course result," "personal interaction," and "instructor effort." A revised fourteen-item form of the rating sheet was constructed, with which it was planned to do a more elaborate analysis involving much larger samples.

CRANNELL, C. W. "An Experiment in the Rating of Instructors by Their Students." *College and University,* 1948, *24,* 5–11.

The article presents data obtained in the College of Arts and

Science at Miami University during the fall semester of 1947–1948 when all students in every course made anonymous ratings of each of their instructors. This procedure was followed: the sheets were passed out, and while the students were occupied in filling them out, the class instructor either sat at his desk and read or stood and looked out of the window; a student in the class then collected the sheets, shuffled them, and placed them in an envelope which then was sealed; at the conclusion of the class hour, this envelope was taken at once to the office of the chairman; after all grades for the semester had been turned in, the chairman opened the envelopes and inspected the sheets before returning them to each instructor concerned. In summary, this instructor rating procedure was favorably received by students and faculty alike; members of the faculty probably profited by the direct exposure to student opinion—how else shall a teacher attain any immediate information concerning his success with students?; and any "danger" of damage to an instructor's reputation through the uncontrolled, anonymous attacks of a "disgruntled minority" is certainly far from evident in these data.

CRAWFORD, P. L., AND BRADSHAW, H. L. "Perception of Characteristics of Effective University Teachers: A Scaling Analysis." *Educational and Psychological Measurement,* 1968, *28,* 1079–1085.

From an analysis of three hundred student themes describing university teacher characteristics which they considered essential to "effective teaching," thirteen different descriptive statements emerged. These descriptions were randomly arranged for paired comparison scaling and were presented to 158 students, fifty faculty, and thirty administrators and department chairmen. Scale values were computed for the thirteen descriptive statements for each of the ten groups. Statistically significant coefficients of agreement were found, which indicate perceptual agreement among the judges within each group. Comparisons of each group of judgments with the "population" sample revealed significant differences between the values of descriptive statements assigned by different groups of judges. The authors concluded that characteristics of effective teachers may be quantified and studied scientifically but that these characteristics should be interpreted only in light of who is doing the judging.

CREAGER, J. A. "A Multiple-Factor Analysis of the Purdue Rating Scale for Instructors." In H. H. Remmers (Ed.), *Studies in Higher Education: Studies in College and University Staff Evaluation*. Lafayette, Ind.: Purdue University, The Division of Educational Reference, 1950.

This study was designed as a factorial exploration of college students' perceptions of their instructors in terms of ten traits given in the Purdue Rating Scale for Instructors (PRSI). The sampling was directed to 4,147 students and sixty-five instructors. A comparison of this study and a previous one carried out under different conditions showed "remarkable stability" in the factor pattern. The PRSI is not a direct and objective measure of the instructors' personality traits; rather, it measures ways in which students perceive the traits of their instructors; and the students' answers may be conceived as being neither wholly objective nor wholly subjective. If students' perceptions are influenced by their affective responses to the instructor, this very affectivity is at stake in the classroom situation, and the realization of it concerns the thoughtful instructor. Are the measurements valid? If this view of what the scale purports to measure is accepted, then validity may be considered as synonymous with reliability.

CRONBACH, L. J. "Evaluation for Course Improvement." In R. C. Anderson, and others (Eds.), *Current Research on Instruction*. Englewood Cliffs, N.J.: Prentice-Hall, 1969.

While the author deals primarily with the elementary and secondary school levels, several of his ideas are relevant to the post secondary level. He writes that evaluation is used in making three types of decisions: Course improvement—deciding what instructional materials and methods are satisfactory and where change is needed; decisions about individuals—identifying the needs of the pupil for the sake of planning his instruction, judging pupil merit for purposes of selection and grouping, and acquainting the pupil with his own progress and deficiencies; and administrative regulation —judging how good the school system is, how good individual teachers are, and so forth. When evaluation is carried out for course improvement, the chief aim is to find out the effects of the course, that is, what changes it produces in pupils. An aim to compare one course with another should not dominate plans for course evaluation. The author defines evaluation as the collection and use of information to make decisions about an educational program.

CUNEO, P. (Ed.) "Are These Criteria for Hiring and Firing Faculty the Same as Yours?" *College Management,* 1972, *7,* 16–20.

A University of Chicago committee on the Criteria of Academic Appointment reports its criteria for assessing faculty, the essence of which is as follows: "The standards to be applied by any appointive body should be those which assess the quality of performance in (1) research; (2) teaching and training, including the supervision of graduate students; (3) contribution to intellectual community; and (4) services." These criteria are listed in order of importance. Nine college presidents from various sizes and types of institutions responded to the Chicago statement.

DAUGHERTY, H. A. "Appraising College Teachers." *Improving College and University Teaching,* 1968, *16,* 203–206.

The author examines the difficult problems arising from the necessity of evaluating teaching at the college level: should research ability or scholarly productivity be evaluated; how and on what bases is evaluation made; what are the measurable objectives; who should make the evaluation; and what use is made of evaluation? The article addresses itself to these questions, quoting from various authors and studies.

DE BRIUM, H. C. "Quality Instruction." *Improving College and University Teaching,* 1967, *15,* 214–215.

Two hundred sixty-eight graduate students were asked to rate an instructor's overall ability and also to check whether the instructor exhibited any of ten "observed instructor self-concepts" such as good perception of subject matter, sensitivity to individual needs, belief in students' ability to learn, enthusiasm, self confidence, etc. Two of the ten characteristics—helps rather than dictates, and evidence of wholesome family life—bore no relation to the overall ratings.

DESHPANDE, A. S., AND OTHERS. "Student Perceptions of Engineering Instructor Behaviors and Their Relationships to the Evaluation of Instructors and Courses." *American Educational Research Journal,* 1970, 7, 289–305.

The study included 674 undergraduate students who rated thirty-two engineering teachers. Intercorrelations among 147 engineering teacher behavior items were factor analyzed and fourteen interpretable first-order factors were extracted. These factors, in order of listed frequency, were: motivation, rapport, structure, clarity, content mastery, overload (too much work required), evaluation procedure, use of teaching aids, instructional skills, and teaching styles. The results indicated that student ratings of teacher classroom behavior are fairly reliable and that certain dimensions of these behaviors are systematically related to the judged quality of the instructor's teaching efforts and the value of the course.

DETCHEN, L. "Shall the Student Rate the Professor?" *The Journal of Higher Education,* 1940, *11,* 146–154.

The student does have an opinion about faculty which he will record sincerely if given the opportunity. His opinion can help contribute toward a better planning for his welfare and is desirable because it supplements the opinion of the expert. It would be an error to test the validity of student opinion with that of the expert because the expert cannot judge the teacher's affect upon the student; only the student can know this. In studies made at the University of Louisville, negligible differences were found in the rating patterns of A and B students and D and F students, and negligible differences were found among the different grade levels of students. It is equally important to win faculty as well as student cooperation in the rating to prevent the faculty from influencing student opinion by either their words or attitudes.

DE VANE, W. C. "The Role of the Dean of the College." In A. J. Dibden (Ed.), *The Academic Deanship in American Colleges and Universities.* Carbondale, Ill.: Southern Illinois University Press, 1968.

DOWNIE, N. W. "Student Evaluation of Faculty." *Journal of Higher Education,* 1952, *23,* 495–503.

A number of findings from student evaluation data developed at the State College of Washington are presented. They are based upon 16,000 analyzed student forms for classes of 406 instructors. On grade point average, above and below 3.0, only one item—how well course objectives were met—was rated less favorably by above 3.0 students; twelve of the items were rated less favorably by those below 3.0. On elective and required courses, only slight differences were evident, with students in elective courses rating higher the organization and presentation of the material, the laboratory work, and the adequacy of the job done by the teacher. On upper and lower division students, upper-division students rated a few items more favorably than did those in lower division: these were opportunity to discuss tests, introduction of new materials, influence of course on taking another course in the same area, value of laboratories, and arousal of intellectual curiosity. On class size, with over thirty considered as a large class, a preference was found for smaller classes. In the large classes the instructional procedures, tests and quizzes, and the value of the course received less favorable ratings, while in smaller classes the instructor-student relations received harsher ratings. On age of teacher, no differences were found between the over- and under-forty age groups. On rank of teacher, most of the differences appeared in the area of teacher-student relations where full professors were rated highest. All three professorial ranks were rated higher than were instructors on knowledge of subject matter, but instructors marked and returned tests more promptly than did assistant and full professors. On degree held by teacher, those with the two highest degrees had better organized courses, more effective presentations, and gave more appropriate assignments than did those with only the bachelor's degree. Also, those with the doctor's degree knew their subject better, better stimulated intellectual curiosity, and did a more adequate teaching job. On sex of teacher, women were rated more favorably on the extent to which new books were drawn to the students' attention; otherwise there were no differences. And on length of service at the institution, no differences were found between those who had been employed more or less than five years.

DRESSEL, P. L., JOHNSON, F. C., AND MARCUS, P. M. *The Confidence Crisis: An Analysis of University Departments.* San Francisco: Jossey-Bass, 1970.

DRESSEL, P. L. "Evaluation of the Environment, the Process, and the Results of Higher Education." In A. S. Knowles (Ed.), *Handbook of College and University Administration: Academic.* New York: McGraw-Hill, 1970.

Evaluation or planning of instruction must start from some accepted statement of the responsibilities of instruction, for example: motivating the student; demonstrating to the student what new knowledge, behavior, or reactions are expected from him; providing extensive and meaningful materials; providing knowledge about his performance and the satisfaction of progress where possible, organizing the work well; and providing the student with high standards and

with means for judging the extent to which his performance
meets these standards. The author believes that systematic
evaluation of instruction is essential, for at least three reasons: it is required for the recognition and reward of good
instruction; it provides knowledge and understanding which
make possible improved instruction and learning; and it
helps psychological and educational researchers understand
the nature of learning. All three reasons ultimately condense
into one: the improvement of the educational process. The
most common systematic approach to the evaluation of instruction is through student evaluation. The evidence, while
not completely consistent, indicates that grades of students
do not have great impact on their ratings. The recent surge
of student-conducted appraisal of teaching is of dubious
value with respect to the improvement of instruction. Peer
and administrative evaluations of instruction are also made,
whether or not they are formerly structured, and these informal appraisals are based on very inadequate evidence,
seldom recorded and therefore difficult to contest. Every
new junior faculty member should be visited by the department chairman or another faculty member who can assist
him in the many adjustments of a new situation. Self-evaluation is essential to improvement. Until an individual confronts his professional weaknesses with a mind to improve,
evaluation will be resented and rejected. Another way to
evaluate instruction is by measuring the achievement of students. For example, if students of a given teacher regularly
excel or regularly fall below the mean performance of the
group, some judgments may reasonably be made about the
capabilities of that teacher.

DRESSEL, P. L. "Evaluation of Instruction." *Journal of Farm Economics,* 1967, *49,* 299.

Student ratings have been found to be fairly consistent, regardless of grade or class level. Yet, due to the instructor's
displeasure with the process, it may be more realistic to have
the students engage in a broader type of evaluation in refer-

ence to the course or the total learning experience. Observation by peers or by administrative superiors is regularly practiced by some institutions and probably should be more common. Good instruction depends upon curriculum organization and the facilities available, upon objectives, methods, and materials, and upon how these are organized and interrelated.

DRESSEL, P. L. "Teaching, Learning and Evaluation." In H. A. Estrin and D. M. Goode (Eds.), *College and University Teaching.* Dubuque, Iowa: William Brown Co., 1964.

Evaluation and instruction in learning are inseparable, and both implicit and explicit objectives should coincide to allow for meaningful objectives. Rational determination of objectives requires consideration of change in amount and direction. Evaluation all too often emphasizes errors and ignores strengths. Instruction requires providing opportunities for the student to practice behavior stated in faculty objectives. Students should recognize shared responsibility for effectiveness, and evaluation should be learned experience for both teacher and student.

DRESSEL, P. L., AND ASSOCIATES. *Evaluation in Higher Education.* Boston: Houghton Mifflin, 1961.

This book contains thirteen chapters, written by various authorities, which follow this pattern: chapters One to Three consider successively the nature and role of evaluation, the significance and the problems of defining educational objectives, and the relationship of evaluation to the learning process; chapters Four to Seven treat specific evaluation and testing problems in the four broad areas of social science, the natural sciences, the humanities, and communications. Chapters Eight and Nine are closely related to the previous four chapters; and chapters Ten to Thirteen consider the nature and role of evaluation in several phases of institutional planning and policy determination.

DRESSEL, P. L. "The Essential Nature of Evaluation." In P. L. Dressel and Associates, *Evaluation in Higher Education*. Boston: Houghton Mifflin, 1961.

The nature, extent, and role of evaluation practices in any institution depend on the educational philosophies of the faculty, the administration, and, to some extent, the constituency supporting the institution. Three contrasting patterns of thinking about education are identified: the *traditionalist,* oriented primarily to the past, holds that evaluation must be highly subjective, emphasizing oral and written procedures which are cumulative and comprehensive in nature; and evaluation as a basis for determination of educational policy is unlikely to lean very much on data collection or other empirical procedures. The *eclectic,* oriented to the present, tends to focus on mastery of a body of factual knowledge and possibly upon the intellectual skills needed; and cumulative, comprehensive evaluation is deemed of little worth because courses and disciplines stand as separates with little planned relationship. Most colleges operate on an eclectic basis. The *relativist,* oriented to the future, contends that evaluation is not simply a basis for decisions; it is in itself a significant and necessary educational experience. Dressel considers evaluation as both a means and an end. As a means, it includes studies and procedures designed to maintain or to improve the quality of instruction or of learning. As an end, it refers to improved thought, which is the most frequently expressed single objective for higher education. For this reason, it was chosen as the culminating category in the hierarchical ordering of cognitive objectives developed by B. Bloom. (*Taxonomy of Education Objectives*. New York: Longmans, Green, 1956.)

DRESSEL, P. "The Current Status of Research on College and University Teaching." In W. J. McKeachie (Ed.), *The Appraisal of Teaching in Large Universities*. Ann Arbor, Mich.: The University of Michigan Extension Service, 1959.

Several criteria for evaluating teaching effectiveness are outlined: correlation of student ability measured and grades received; delayed measures of retention, which emphasize mastery rather than cramming; quality of work in later courses in a sequentially organized discipline; the number of majors attracted to a department as a result of taking a first course; classroom observation by peers or by supervisors; student growth as measured by pre- and posttesting; student appraisal of instructors; and impacts on the profession and on one's associates. The desire of the administrator to use objective and defensible evidence related to teaching raises the element of threat to the faculty member, which may interfere with instructional improvement of those who are threatened. Attempts to evaluate instruction on some uniform basis must give way to programs to encourage instructors to improve, each in the way best suited to him, to his field, to his purpose, and to his students.

DRESSEL, P. L., AND MAYHEW, L. V. *General Education: Explorations in Evaluation.* Washington, D.C.: American Council on Education, 1954.

The authors identify three professional attitudes toward evaluation. One completely rejects evaluation other than the judgment of the teachers themselves, contending that many instructional outcomes are intangible and are assessable only by an instructor who is in close contact with a student over a period of time. Rejection of evaluation is particularly common among humanities teachers. Subjectively, it seems that a majority of this group are also strongly content-oriented in the actual conduct of their courses. A second group of teachers recognizes the need for evaluation but feels that the exigencies of teaching make it impossible to do much about results. The size of classes, the teaching load, and the amount of material to be covered are given as factors that force teachers into the use of formal and traditional instructional procedures which are not particularly conducive to student development other than in factual knowledge. Science and social science teachers are likely to be found in this second group. A third group, which is increasing in numbers, has had formal measurement and evaluation training and experience, and members are generally supportive but often critical of evaluative efforts. There would seem to be a positive but not perfect correlation between active interest in the broader problems of evaluation and concern for introduction of a greater degree of student orientation into the general education program.

DRESSEL, P. L. "Faculty Development, Appraisal, and Reward." Unpublished document. Michigan State University, n.d.

Six major areas of faculty activity are discussed: professional competence and professional activity (scholarship and advanced study, research, professional activity); curriculum planning and evaluation; classroom teaching (planning of instruction, evaluation, effective communication, evaluation of teaching); academic advising of students; public service; and faculty statesmanship. Faculty evaluation is not merely a matter of looking at instruction or research; faculty development involves a determination of what each person can do best and the utilization of these talents.

DRUCKER, A. J., AND REMMERS, H. H. "Do Alumni and Students Differ in Their Attitudes Toward Instructors?" In H. H. Remmers (Ed.), *Studies in Higher Education: Studies in College and University Staff Evaluation*. Lafayette, Ind.: Purdue University, The Division of Educational Reference, 1950.

To test the hypothesis that ratings of instructors do not change with the maturity of the rater, comparisons were made of the ratings of ninety-two Purdue University instructors by 138 alumni (of at least ten years standing) with ratings by 251 current undergraduates. The relative importance of the ten traits of the Purdue Rating Scale for Instructors to alumni and students was also examined. The study reached these conclusions: there are substantial positive relationships between the relative average ratings of instructors by students and alumni; the average differences that do occur between student and alumni ratings of Purdue University instructors indicate that present students as a group rate their instructors slightly higher than they will when they are older but that such differences are too small to be significant; Purdue University students and alumni agree highly upon the relative importance to good instruction of the ten traits of the Purdue Rating Scale for Instructors.

EASTMAN, A. M. "How Visitation Came to Carnegie-Mellon University." In K. E. Eble, *The Recognition and Evaluation of Teaching.* Salt Lake City: Project to Improve College Teaching, 1259 East South Temple, 1970. (Reprinted from *Bulletin of the Association of Departments of English,* May, 1969.)

This case study tells about the trials and tribulations of a new chairman of the English Department at Carnegie-Mellon. He came to a department that did not visit its teachers from a department that did. The article provides a detailed account of the interdynamics of how classroom visitation was initiated at Carnegie-Mellon.

EBLE, K. E. *Professors as Teachers.* San Francisco, Jossey-Bass, 1972.

The book draws upon observations and conclusions derived from a two-year Project to Improve College Teaching, jointly sponsored by AAUP and the Association of American Colleges, but the author goes beyond what is found in his other reports of the Project. The book offers a series of positive proposals which are designed to improve college instruction, to reward teaching excellence, and to revitalize undergraduate education through renewed interest in teaching. Chapter subjects are: professors in the classroom, attitudes toward teaching, teaching effectively, evaluating teaching, what students want, learning to teach, faculty development, rewards of teaching, the teaching environment, is teaching obsolete?, and an epilogue: professors as teachers. A selected bibliography is included.

EBLE, K. E. *The Recognition and Evaluation of Teaching.* Salt Lake City: Project to Improve College Teaching, 1259 East South Temple, 1970.

This small book is an essential work for those interested in this field. Its contents include: recognition of teaching, evaluation and the improvement of teaching, student evaluation instruments and procedures, impact of student evaluation, and faculty review. The appendix contains detailed information on the course evaluation procedures at Princeton University and the University of Washington, and a case study of classroom visitation at Carnegie-Mellon University. A useful bibliography is included. The book is the first report of the two-year Project to Improve College Teaching.

EBLE, K. E. "Project to Improve College Teaching." *Academe,* 1970, *4,* 3–6.

A two-year study jointly sponsored by the AAUP and the Association of American Colleges is described. It was designed as a career development study and begins with methods for attracting talented persons into the profession; it follows their development as college teachers and concludes with a consideration of how to maintain teaching effectiveness throughout a faculty member's career. "Evaluation" is the major topic.

ECHANDIA, P. P. "A Methodological Study and Factor Analytic Validation of Forced-Choice Performance Ratings of College Accounting Instructors." *Dissertation Abstracts,* 1964, *25*(4)ˈ, 2605–2606.

The main purpose of this study was to determine whether the criteria students use for judging effective teaching are the same ones they use when they rate instructors. The

sample consisted of 546 students and sixteen accounting instructors. The factor analysis of the intercorrelations among
the forced-choice items produced four factors: (1) the
ability to communicate the subject on a level the students
understand; (2) the ability to deal with students, assignments, and grades appropriately; (3) the ability to motivate
students; and (4) the ability to anticipate and forestall difficulties students may encounter with the subject. Low com-
monality was found among the four factors, caused by high
specific and/or error variance. The forced-choice rating
device differentiated between the best and poorest but not
between the best and average instructors.

ECKERT, R. E., AND KELLER, R. J. "Student Ratings of College
Teaching." In Eckert and Keller (Eds.), *A University Looks
at Its Program*. Minneapolis: The University of Minnesota
Press, 1954.

A student appraisal instrument was given to almost fifteen
thousand students enrolled in 380 courses in the College of
Science, Literature, and the Arts at the University of Minnesota in the winter of 1949. Anonymity of students was insured, and each instructor's rating was disclosed only to
himself. The emphasis of the rating scale was diagnostic
rather than pointed toward evaluating general teaching
effectiveness. The instrument was administered by two student groups during the last three weeks of the quarter. Student assistance worked well. The rating scales were collected
by the student assistant, sealed in the presence of the class
and the instructor who remained in the room. On a detach-
able tab clipped to this envelope were written the name of
the instructor, the department, and the course. These envelopes were given to a selected graduate student who removed
the tab and coded the information so these data could be
used for research purposes. Analyses found very little relationship between student grades and ratings, except for students below C, who gave their instructors a higher mean
rating in general teaching ability than did students report-

ing grades higher than C. A direct relationship was found to exist between the quality of ratings received and the rank of the instructor, with professors and associate professors consistently receiving higher scores; instructors in humanities and natural sciences seemed to be more favorably regarded than were those in the social studies; seniors and graduate students gave higher ratings than did lower classmen; classes of intermediate size (between forty and two hundred) developed less rapport with students than did the small or large classes; and classes held during the middle of the day received higher ratings than did early morning ones, which in turn were regarded more favorably than were late afternoon classes. A survey that included 132 instructors who had used the instrument found general satisfaction with the rating scale, and a majority (62 percent) believed the information provided to the instructor was quite useful.

ECKERT, R. E. "Ways of Evaluating College Teaching." *School and Society*, 1950, *71*, 65–69.

Recognizing that the strength of any school or college depends basically on the competence and devotion of its faculty, educators are seeking to identify—and ultimately measure—those characteristics that help to make an institution great. The ideal way to appraise a teacher's effectiveness would be to study comprehensively the impact of his instruction upon students in his classes, but it is impossible to wait five or ten years to decide whether one teacher's contract should be renewed or whether another teacher should be promoted. The author gives some bases upon which teaching competence can be appraised: inspection of the materials developed for courses; observation of participation in college discussions and committee work focused on teaching problems; published materials bearing on teaching problems; participation in state, regional, and national associations; regular and systematic class visitation; student ratings; comparisons of standings secured on departmental examinations by students in various sections taught by different instructors; comparisons of students' performance on pre- and post-tests; studies of the activities in which students engage while they are taking the course in question; and investigations of the subsequent activities of students, particularly in the first few years after they have taken a given course or a sequence of courses. The importance to be attached to these various types of evidence will depend on several factors; no neat mathematical formula will provide a ready answer to the question of which teachers are the most effective in a given institution.

EDUCATIONAL TESTING SERVICE. *Student Instructional Report* (SIR). Princeton, N.J.: The Service, 1971.

As stated in its descriptive flyer, the purpose of SIR is to improve instruction. It gives the instructor an opportunity to monitor his own performance and progress, and it provides the student with an opportunity to express his views of the course and the way in which it was taught. The content and format of the Student Instructional Report are not permanent or fixed; they will be modified and updated regularly to reflect changes in teaching and in students. A core of items will remain the same, but new items will be added based on the results of ongoing research studies, suggestions from faculty and students, and continued experience with SIR. Colleges and universities that use SIR receive a summary report for each class, which indicates the percentage of students who chose various response options to each question and the average (mean) response. Each class is summarized on a separate, three-page report.

EDWARDS, C. N. "The Performance Rating: A Study in Teacher Evaluation." *Educational and Psychological Measurement*, 1968, *28*, 487–492.

Medical nursing instructors, operating room instructors, and psychiatric instructors in five nursing schools were asked to rate fifty-five senior nursing students on their performance in three types of nursing situations: medical care, operating room, and psychiatric nursing. Both Pearson and interclass correlation coefficients among instructor ratings of students in the three types of situations were of low magnitude, with none of the correlations accounting for more than 3 percent of the variance. Performance ratings were also found to correlate .27 or less, with test scores in the corresponding nursing speciality. Nursing practice grades awarded by the instructors in their respective specialities correlated .49 or less, with their ratings of the students' performance in situations characteristic of the speciality.

ELLIOTT, D. N. "Characteristics and Relationships of Various Criteria of College and University Teaching." In H. H. Remmers (Ed.), *Studies in Higher Education: Studies in College and University Staff Evaluation.* Lafayette, Ind.: Purdue University, The Division of Educational Reference, 1950.

The investigation of various criteria of teaching are reported in two studies. The first study delved into 26,014 student ratings of 460 teachers and also into teacher knowledge of correct teaching practices involving mental hygiene practices ($N = 342$). Some conclusions supported by the data are as follows: The sex of the teacher is not reflected by the ratings given by students. Female teachers have a better knowledge of correct teaching practices involving mental hygiene principles than do male teachers. Teachers with the least academic rank received somewhat lower student ratings; beyond the lowest academic rank, ratings were not systematically related to increasing rank except for three traits—presentation of subject matter, self-reliance and confidence, and stimulation of intellectual curiosity. Differences in teaching rank and experience were not related to knowledge of correct teaching procedures involving mental hygiene principles.

The second study, involving thirty-six instructors in a required general chemistry course for freshman engineering majors, made interesting conclusions. Those teachers willing to express the strongest opinions concerning correct teaching procedures are poorer in terms of student achievement than are those less willing to express strong opinions. Knowledge of chemistry among graduate chemistry students who teach elementary chemistry courses is negatively related to achievement of their students. Teachers whose students achieved relatively more, regardless of student ability, received relatively higher ratings from their students. Grades per se were not related to ratings given teachers by their students. Subject matter knowledge is not related to student ratings. In terms of student achievement, some instructors are more effective with high-ability students than they are with low-ability students; others are of more help to low-ability students.

ENARSON, H. L. "University or Knowledge Factory?" *The Chronicle of Higher Education,* 1973, 7, 16.

ESTRIN, H. A., AND GODWIN, L. R. "Evaluating English Teaching." *Improving College and University Teaching,* 1962, *10,* 193–196.

Students of Newark College of Engineering have been evaluating their teachers for seventeen years. The program is conducted by Tau Beta Pi engineering honor society, with institutional approval, and when invited by a faculty member. It is confidential and involves coding, charting of overall results, and is followed by the burning of data sheets. Each instructor receives an individual report. By comparing his own with the composite report, he can determine how he compares with his colleagues. Since neither his colleagues nor the administration have access to the ratings, the evaluation serves a single purpose—improvement of instruction. Class visitation usually involves the department head, who observes a class three times during an instructor's year of tenure. The first visit is in the nature of orientation; the second, for evaluation of the teaching; and the third, to summarize and confirm the observations made during the second visit.

EVANS, R. I. *Resistance to Innovation in Higher Education.* San Francisco: Jossey-Bass, 1968.

FAHEY, G. L. "Student Rating of Teaching: Some Questionable Assumptions." In Alex J. Ducanis, *Student Evaluation of Teaching.* Pittsburgh, Pa.: Institute for Higher Education, University of Pittsburgh, 1970.

Several assumptions are analyzed that relate to evaluation of teaching. Stating that he is not against scales for students to rate teachers, the author contends that they are probably more objecive, reliable, and perhaps are more valid than are any alternative procedure which we now use for such assessment. He raises several cautions in using them: they yield pooled reactions to those dimensions which were built into the scale; they presume uniformity of conditions, styles, and purposes; they are shaped by statistical treatment not to be additive to single scores; they are interpretable only against ideals of which no model has consensus, or against norms which may or may not be appropriate; they have an influence on teacher-student relations which is unknown; and they have a built-in predisposition to establish models to be copied.

FARRAR, W. E. "Dimensions of Faculty Performance as Perceived by Faculty." *Dissertation Abstracts,* 1969, *29*(10a), 3458-A.

A study at the University of Houston used a questionnaire to identify factors descriptive of the faculty member's role as faculty members see it. Based upon responses from eighty-seven faculty members, the factors, in order of the percentage of variance for which they account, were: classroom teaching skill, research and writing competency, responsible cooperation, community involvement, and orientation toward improvement.

FENKER, R., AND SECREST, L. "Teacher Evaluation at Texas Christian University: An Analysis of the Perceived Roles of Faculty by Students, Administrators, and Faculty." Unpublished paper, 1972.

As a result of a self-study program, Texas Christian University (TCU) embarked on a full-scale evaluation project. Its basic goals were to improve the university by recognizing and rewarding "excellence" in all aspects of administrator and faculty behavior and to reduce the arbitrariness of the decision-making processes associated with promotions, tenure, and raises by making the goals and reward structure more explicit. Utilizing the available literature on evaluation, the following instruments were developed: (1) teacher evaluation, (2) colleague evaluation (for faculty), (3) administrator evaluation, (4) faculty self-evaluation, (5) evaluation forms for professional staff, and (6) a form for evaluating the state of the university. The evaluation instruments were "validated" by having faculty, administrators, and students rate the items on the instruments in terms of their importance to the position being evaluated. This procedure resulted in an enormous body of data on the self-perceptions of various faculty groups and administrators as well as information on what each group of raters (for example, students) considered the most important behaviors in other groups.

Multiple discriminant analysis procedures were used to identify differences in the perceptions of the various groups of raters. These analyses provided considerable insight into the differences between the colleges at TCU with respect to the behaviors considered the "most important." Discrepancies between the faculty's and administrators' "ideal teacher" and the students' "ideal" were also illustrated. Several conclusions regarding evaluation procedures in universities, including the "ape's hand phenomenon" are discussed. (See Chapter Four for details.)

FINKIN, M. W. "Collective Bargaining and University Government." *AAUP Bulletin,* 1971, *57,* 149–162.

FISCHER, J. "Is There a Teacher on the Faculty?" *Harper's,* 1965, *230,* 18–28.

The author declares that the harsh truth is that nearly all of our colleges and universities are capable of providing far better instruction than they actually do. They do not do it simply because our whole academic system is rigged against good teaching. The author provides reasons why so much college teaching is poor: We do not have objective, impersonal methods to measure the quality of teaching. There is no solid, safe yardstick that a dean or department head can use to justify raising the pay of a good instructor, or firing a poor one. Consequently, in doling out rewards and punishments the administrator falls back on something that can be measured: research and publication. A healthy balance between scholarship and teaching probably can never be restored until a reasonably objective yardstick is devised for testing and rewarding performance of the teacher. Another reason for substandard teaching is that college professors do not know how to teach. Students are dissatisfied also because the best professors are seldom home. The public is bound to have an increasing say in the management of higher education. (For a response to Fischer's article, see Hutchinson, W. R.)

FISHMAN, J. "Cross-Cultural Perspective on the Evaluation of Guided Behavioral Change." *The Evaluation of Teaching.* Washington, D.C.: Pi Lambda Theta, 1967.

Examination of the characteristics and behavior of teachers has been the basis of evaluating teaching effectiveness in the United States. Although it is clear that the teacher and his method of teaching are important to the learning process, we cannot yet say just what it is that the effective teacher is or does. Teaching cannot be evaluated independently of learning, nor can learning be evaluated independently of teaching. American teachers must learn to accept evaluation.

FLANAGAN, J. C. "The Critical Incident Technique." *Psychological Bulletin,* 1954, *51,* 327–358.

The critical incident technique consists of a set of procedures for collecting direct observations of human behavior to facilitate their potential usefulness in solving practical problems and developing broad psychological principles. The technique outlines procedures for collecting observed incidents of special significance and which meet systematically defined criteria. The five steps in the procedure are: determination of the general aim of the activity, development of plans and specifications for collecting factual incidents regarding the activity, collection of the data, analysis of the data, and interpretation and reporting of the statement of the requirements of the activity. The technique, rather than collecting opinions, hunches, and estimates, obtains a record of specific behaviors from those in the best position to make the necessary observations and evaluations.

FLETCHER, F. M. "Measuring Teaching Effectiveness Through Evaluating Student Learning." In W. J. McKeachie (Ed.), *The Appraisal of Teaching in Large Universities.* Ann Arbor, Mich.: The University of Michigan Extension Service, 1959.

Clarification of our goals or criteria of teaching is necessary before we can measure effectiveness, and one critical outcome of teaching is the ultimate impact that the course has on the individual. A tentative set of propositions regarding intellectual curiosity is given, with emphasis upon the process of an individual "responding" to the course, followed by "reinforcement" experiences. Each individual is different, and a state of individual readiness must exist for him to respond. We cannot predict accurately who will respond nor exactly when a "potential" individual will respond.

FRENCH, G. M. "College Students' Concept of Effective Teaching Determined by an Analysis of Teacher Ratings." *Dissertation Abstracts,* 1957, *17,* 1380–1381.

The purpose of this investigation undertaken at the University of Washington was to discover what teacher characteristics, measured by a set of verbal statements (items), are related to students' high or low opinions of their college teachers. The 41 items were treated as a set of predictors of the overall judgment. Factor analysis revealed that there are probably not more than eight dimensions to the students' concept of effective teaching, and also it made clear that one of these factors is of much greater importance than all the others. A second factor and possibly a third appear to be of some importance, and the others contribute only in a very minor way. The ten items which contribute most to overall judgment are the following: (1) interprets abstract ideas and theories clearly; (2) gets students interested in the subject; (3) has increased my skills in thinking; (4) has helped broaden my interests; (5) stresses important material; (6) makes good use of examples and illustrations; (7) motivated me to do my best work; (8) inspires class confidence in his knowledge of the subject; (9) has given me new viewpoints or appreciations; and (10) is clear and understandable in his explanations. Five of these items (2, 5, 6, 8, 10) were among the top ten in the studies made by E. R. Guthrie more than a generation ago, when he asked students what characteristics were important to good teaching. These items suggest that student judgments of good teaching are generally stable and do not differ significantly from faculty concepts of good teaching. These data also indicate that neatness of appearance, friendliness of manner, sense of humor, the giving of individual attention, and the handling of examinations carry little weight in the students' descriptions of effective teachers.

GADZELLA, B. M. "College Students' Views and Ratings of an Ideal Professor." *College and University*, 1968, *44*, 89–96.

A questionnaire study made at Western Washington State College (WWSC), Bellingham, of the "ideal professor" included responses from 443 randomly selected students. The five most important criteria were: knowledge of subject (has a thorough knowledge, both basic and current, of the subject he teaches); interest in subject (has a deep interest in and enthusiasm for the subject he teaches); flexibility (is inspiring, has the ability to present material to meet students' interests and needs); daily and course preparations (has daily lessons well organized, provides an outline of the course and its objectives and a list of basic references); and vocabularly (uses appropriate language, has ability to explain clearly, presents material at the students' level of comprehension). In the list of twenty-five characteristics, the five least important criteria were: writer (writes books and articles for journals and publications); participator in community (takes an active part in community life, participates in clubs and community projects); researcher (organizes and/or participates in research); appearance (is well-groomed and appropriately dressed); and punctuality (is punctual for classes). The criteria selected by students at WWSC describe the ideal professor's most important role as teaching and learning; namely, that he is well informed on the subject he teaches, is interested in it, and is able to inspire his students.

GAFF, J. G., AND WILSON, R. C. "Faculty Values and Improving Teaching." In G. K. Smith (Ed.), *New Teaching New Learning*. San Francisco: Jossey-Bass, 1971.

Perhaps the most important institutional policy affecting the motivations of faculty members, according to the authors, is the reward structure, which includes both the distribution of extrinsic rewards and the opportunity for faculty to derive intrinsic satisfactions from their work. The evaluation of teaching is also related to the issue of an adequate reward structure. Teaching evaluation serves two general purposes: it provides teachers with feedback that can help them improve their teaching, and it can give added weight to teaching in the advancement procedures. In order for these benefits to be realized, the methods for assessing the quality of teaching must be both reliable and systematic. However, few colleges have a formal procedure that systematically provides reliable evidence of a professor's teaching effectiveness. Feasible procedures that have been used to obtain systematic evidence of effective teaching include classroom visitation by colleagues, self-assessment, and student ratings.

GAFF, J. G., WILSON, R. C., AND OTHERS. *The Teaching Environment: A Study of Optimum Working Conditions for Effective College Teaching.* Berkeley, Calif.: Center for Research and Development in Higher Education, 1970.

The report includes several sections that bear directly on faculty performance and evaluation: views of teachers, institutional supports for good teaching, relationships with students, relationships with colleagues, reward structure, teaching evaluation, and work load. The authors conclude that: (1) faculty members should be aware of general developments in higher education, especially those developments most directly related to teaching and learning; (2) there should be a visible comprehensive program to assist the personal and professional development of faculty members; (3) there should be provision for faculty members to obtain useful feedback from students concerning their teaching activities; (4) there should be periodic reviews of the instructional program and proposals for its improvement; (5) intelligent efforts to restructure curricula and reform courses are valuable but probably insufficient.

GAFF, J. G., AND WILSON, R. C. "Moving the Faculty." *Change,* 1970, *1,* 10–12.

GAGE, N. L. "The Appraisal of College Teaching." *Journal of Higher Education,* 1961, *32,* 17–22.

Appraisals must be fair; teachers should not be penalized for conditions over which they have no control such as the level of the course, the size of the class, whether the course is elective or required, and where it is taught. Research conducted at the University of Illinois indicated that: (1) teachers of lower level courses had lower ratings than did those of more advanced courses; (2) teachers with a class load of thirty to thirty-nine students had lower ratings than did instructors with fewer students; (3) instructors and assistant professors received lower ratings than did associate professors and professors; (4) off-campus instructors received higher ratings than did on-campus instructors, and (5) teachers of elective courses had higher ratings than did instructors of required courses.

GAGE, N. L. "Ends and Means in Appraising College Teaching." In W. J. McKeachie (Ed.), *The Appraisal of Teaching in Large Universities*. Ann Arbor, Mich.: The University of Michigan Extension Service, 1959.

Teaching is appraised for any of these reasons: as a basis for administrative decisions on academic rank, tenure, and salary; as a basis for self-improvement by teachers; and as a criterion for use in research on teaching. A study of students' ratings of instructors at the University of Illinois found: teachers of lower level courses consistently received less favorable mean ratings than did those of more advanced courses; those of courses with thirty to thirty-nine students consistently received lower ratings than did those of courses with fewer students; instructors and assistant professors consistently received lower ratings than did associate professors and professors; those with on-campus courses received significantly lower ratings than did those with off-campus courses; and teachers of elective courses received consistently more favorable ratings than did those of required courses. How much students learn has obvious strength as a basis for appraising teaching. This approach is usable in large introductory courses of many sections taught by many instructors under uniform conditions such as the same objectives, the same textbooks, the same laboratories, the same class size, and other such considerations.

GARVERICK, C. M., AND CARTER, H. D. "Instructor Ratings and Expected Grades." *California Journal of Educational Research*, 1962, *13*, 218–221.

One hundred and sixty-four students in an introductory educational psychology course at the University of California at Berkeley were involved in this study of whether student ratings of teachers are influenced by the grades that students expect to receive. Based upon a cluster analysis, one cluster composed of items related to expected scholastic grades was found to be almost independent of a second cluster which included items concerned with general instructor effectiveness. It was concluded that no statistically significant relationship was found between the measured ratings of a teacher by students and the grades mentioned as being expected or deserved.

GETZELS, J. W., AND JACKSON, P. W. "The Teacher's Personality and Characteristics." In N. L. Gage (Ed.), *Handbook of Research on Teaching*. Chicago: Rand McNally, 1963.

GIBB, C. A. "Classroom Behavior of the College Teacher." *Educational and Psychological Measurement*, 1955, *15*, 254–263.

Nine teacher behavior description scales were prepared and administered to 119 male students of a liberal arts college. The behavior of seventy different male college teachers, randomly selected was described. Factorial analysis of the resulting correlations between the nine scales resulted in four relatively independent factors or dimensions of teacher behavior. These were designated as: friendly democratic behavior; communication behavior; systematic, organization behavior; and academic emphasis.

GLENNY, L. A. "Reinforcement Trends for State Planning and Systems." Address delivered at the Annual Meeting of the American Association of Colleges, San Francisco, Jan. 15, 1973.

GOODE, D. M. "Evaluation and Teaching." *Journal of Dental Education,* 1967, *30,* 260–264.

The author emphasizes that a profession, such as dentistry, can exist only if it rests on a theory or technology. Evaluation is an ongoing process of identifying and defining values. Visitation, testing procedures, and appraisal by students should be utilized in evaluative techniques.

GOODE, D. M. *72 College Teaching Procedures.* Corvallis, Ore.: Oregon State University Press, 1966.

The author briefly describes seventy-two procedures for increasing the effectiveness of college teaching. These procedures strengthen teacher competence and therefore provide the instructor with better ratings on evaluation.

GOODHARTZ, A. S. "Student Attitudes and Opinions Relating to Teaching at Brooklyn College." *School and Society,* 1948, *68,* 345–349.

Over 90 percent (6,681) of the students at Brooklyn College rated each of their five teachers in May 1947. Two fundamental aims were set up for this investigation: to provide each instructor with a report of his pedagogical stature as measured by his students, and to determine the relationship between the ideals of good teaching as established by the student and the realization of these ideals. The survey was done by a research unit off campus. Each student responded to materials in an envelope, sealed the envelope, and personally deposited it in a large receptacle in the office of the dean of studies. Several findings emerged. For example, when students rated the importance of attributes and factors as they related to the arts, science, and social science, the differences among the three areas were considerable. In general, it was found that critical judgment of the teachers varied in direct ratio with the student's level of scholarship; on every attribute, except knowledge of subject, the better scholars turned in the more critical evaluations, but the range of differences among ratings of good, average, and poor scholars was not great—not more than six points on a 0–100 scale. The survey indicated that teaching quality bears little relationship to the size of class. A small class (under twenty students) does not necessarily result in a more favorable teacher rating than does a large class. Furthermore, there is no conclusive evidence for believing that the ratings given to an instructor are affected by the fact that the course he teaches is an elective or prescribed course, or by such factors as the student's sex or college class. When rated by age, the students clearly rated the twenty to thirty-nine age group ahead of the forty to forty-nine and fifty to sixty-nine group, with the exception of one trait—knowledge of subject.

GRAY, C. E. "The Teaching Model and Evaluation of Teaching Performance." *Journal of Higher Education*, 1969, *40*, 636–642.

A model of the skills and strategies involved in teaching is given. Teacher behavior is thought of as linguistic, performative, and expressive, with these six skills and strategies involved in the teaching act: initiating teacher behavior designed to motivate the learner and give meaning and direction to learning; expository-communicating teacher behavior designed to afford the student the opporunity of acquiring new knowledge; consolidating teacher behavior designed to elicit and reinforce student responses which are indicative of convergent or analytic thinking; consolidating teacher behavior designed to elicit and reinforce student responses which are indicative of divergent or creative thinking; consolidating teacher behavior designed to elicit and reinforce student responses which are indicative of evaluative thinking; and strategic teacher behavior designed to create an educational climate wherein students are willing to attend classes and find satisfaction in doing so. The author also provides twelve criteria for evaluating certain observable aspects of teaching performance.

GUETZKOW, H., AND OTHERS. "An Experimental Comparison of Recitation, Discussion, and Tutorial Methods in College Teaching." *The Journal of Educational Psychology,* 1954, *45,* 193–207.

An experiment in three different teaching methods (drill-recitation, group discussion, and study-tutorial) involved eight of twenty-four sections of an elementary general psychology course at the University of Michigan. By and large, no differences in outcome were found among the teaching methods. The few statistical differences in general favored the recitation-drill method. The results clearly confirm the general conclusion derived from experiments on instructional procedures since the early 1920s. Good wrote: "The complexity of the teaching-learning process is such that attempts to establish the relative merit of a 'general method' of teaching are likely to prove inconclusive." (GOOD, C. V. "Colleges and Universities: VIII. Methods of Teaching." In W. S. Monroe [Ed.], *Encyclopedia of Educational Research.* New York: Macmillan, 1952. Pp. 273–278.)

GUILD, R. "Criterion Problem in Instructor Evaluation." *Journal of Dental Education,* 1967, *30,* 270–279.

The need common to measurement is for a criterion with which the to-be-measured phenomenon can be compared. Criteria that could be used for the evaluation of dental instructors could be formulated under the headings of code of instructional ethics; position description, significant working relations with others, specific work, job knowledge, technical knowledge of teaching and learning; student opinion; and student achievement.

GUSTAD, J. W. "Evaluation of Teaching Performance: Issues and Possibilities." In C. B. T. Lee (Ed.), *Improving College Teaching.* Washington, D.C.: American Council on Education, 1967.

Major trends abstracted from a comparative analysis of the 1961 and 1966 surveys conducted by the American Council on Education are listed. These trends indicate: decline in the use of systematic student ratings; decline in classroom visitation; greater utilization of committee evaluation; greater analysis of grade distributions; wide use of informal student opinions, and evaluation by deans and chairmen; and almost total absence of research on the validity of the instruments used.

GUSTAD, J. W. *Policies and Practices in Faculty Evaluation.* Washington, D.C.: Committee on College Teaching, American Council on Education, 1961. Also in *Educational Record,* 1961, *42,* 194–211.

A study of evaluation practices in 584 institutions was conducted. In the large majority of cases, those principally responsible for evaluation were the president, the dean, and the department (or division) chairman. Of the factors considered in making evaluations, all seven types of institutions studied said that classroom teaching was the most important. Other factors mentioned in order of frequency were: personal attributes, student advising, research, publication, committee work, professional society activity, length of service in rank, public service, supervision of graduate study, consultation, competing offers, and supervision of honors.

Six sources of data most frequently used for evaluating classroom teaching were: informal student opinion; formal student opinion (student ratings); classroom visitation; colleagues' opinions; and the opinions of chairmen and deans.

The faculty resume was the most frequently mentioned source for evaluating research and publications; other frequently mentioned sources were the opinions of colleagues, chairmen, and deans. At least one-half of the institutions stated that they were dissatisfied with their present evaluation policies.

GUTHRIE, E. R. *The Evaluation of Teaching: A Progress Report.* Seattle: University of Washington, 1954.

Studies of evaluation of teaching on the basis of faculty and student judgments have been carried on continuously at the University of Washington since 1924. Various analyses of data collected over these years were used by the author in providing evidence on twelve questions that relate to faculty evaluation: (1) On consistency of student judgments: the considerable diversity of student judgments of a person becomes a very stable measure when the mean of twenty-five judgments is paired with the mean of another twenty-five; over a period of years in which methods and skills of administration have improved, the reliability of a sample of twenty-five surveys has increased from .87 to .94. (2) On agreement of undergraduate and gradute student judgments: underclassmen and graduate students tend to agree strongly (.73) in their overall evaluations of teaching effectiveness. (3) On student and colleague agreement: one hundred twenty-one of the colleague ratings were by means of a nine-item questionnaire. On the first item, teaching effectiveness, the correlation with the annual standing was .43. Ninety-nine of the faculty had been rated by colleagues on a three-item scale with which student evaluations correlated .63. (4) On class size: there is very little if any relation between size of class and rating assigned to the instructor. (5) On judgments of majors and nonmajors: in twenty-seven selected classes, each containing between one-third and two-thirds of nonmajors, only the smallest (less than ten students) showed any significant difference. There was no consistent tendency for students to favor the teachers of their major subject. (6) On student grade-point averages: there was no tendency for the better students to assign ratings different from the others. (7) On affect of current student grades: statistical analyses of data indicate no relationship between grades given and student ratings of the teachers. (8) On faults of poor teachers: "belittling" was the feature most often associated with low ratings. Sarcasm and belittling occurred almost not at all in student comments on good teachers. (9) On entertainment versus knowledge: the sixty-two teachers in the top decile of the annual ratings, according to the writer, revealed a certain out-giving interest (not unlike that of an actor or musician) coupled with a friendly interest in students as persons, and, most important, an industry and interest in the subject which insured preparation for every class period. (10) On experience and teaching effectiveness: there was no relationship. (11) On professorial rank: except for the fact that instructors ranked significantly below associate professors (the next lower rank) and below assistant professors also, there was a very slight improvement from the lower to the upper ranks. (12) On relationship between research and teaching: there is very little relation between colleague ratings on research productivity and student ratings of teaching effectiveness.

GUTHRIE, E. R. "The Evaluation of Teaching." *The Educational Record*, 1949, *30*, 109–115.

First, the author outlines the advantages of merit salary increments, citing a faculty poll taken at the University of Washington which indicated strong support for the merit approach. Further elaboration is given to the faculty evaluation system developed at that university, and initial findings of some research are reported: student ratings do not agree closely with faculty ratings (the correlation is .48 between student-ratings and faculty-jury scores); in the opinion of students, full professors are not better teachers than are assistant professors, while faculty members believe full professors are better. If students are right, the advantages of greater maturity and experience may be offset by possible loss of enthusiasm, increasing distractions, and nonteaching responsibilities.

GUTHRIE, E. R. "Evaluation of Faculty Service." *AAUP Bulletin*, 1945, *31*, 255–262.

The author describes a procedure developed at the University of Washington for evaluating faculty service. The procedure used optional student ratings and rating by a faculty committee. The final step of the system places in the hands of the administrative authority an abstract of colleagues' judgments in the form of an average rating, together with the standard deviation of the ratings which measures the degree of agreement among colleagues. Criteria for promotion were developed from faculty answers to a questionnaire. In order of importance, these criteria were: teaching effectiveness, contribution through research and publication, contribution to university activities, value to the community, ability to cooperate with other members of his department, knowledge of his subject, general knowledge and range of interest, rate of professional growth, and recognition by others in his profession. When the faculty was asked how teaching effectiveness could be measured, 18 percent said this was difficult or impossible. Fifty-two percent of the replies were about equally divided between comments or opinions of colleagues, questionnaires to students, and comments made by students to administrators or other teachers.

HALSTEAD, J. S. "A Model for Research on Ratings of Courses and Instructors." *Proceedings of the 78th Annual Convention of the American Psychological Association,* 1970, 5, 625–626.

The purpose of this study was to demonstrate that the development of adequate rating scales for course and instructor evaluation requires four components: (1) an underlying theory of instruction or a model of the instructional process, (2) a translation of the theory or model into one or more operational definitions, (3) development of a rating scale consistent with the operational definitions, and (4) assurance that the student raters understand the criteria and are skillful observers of the behaviors and processes incorporated in the model.

HAMMOND, P. E., MEYER, J. E., AND MILLER, D. "Teaching versus Research: Sources of Misperceptions." *The Journal of Higher Education,* 1971, 40, 682–689.

In order to clarify the relationship between teaching and research, the authors explore various structural features in academic communities which promote inaccurate perceptions of the central functions of these communities—teaching and research. They are misperceived because of the segmentation of academic communities, leaving each person to form opinions largely from the perspective of his own position.

HARBAUGH, J. W. In private correspondence, 1972.

HARRIS, T. L., AND OTHERS. "Attitudes Expressed by Students Toward a Beginning Course in Educational Psychology." *The Journal of Educational Research,* 1969, *62,* 344–350.

The purpose of this study was to examine the stability of student attitudes toward a beginning course in educational psychology. Measurements occurred at midpoint and the end of the course. Over 350 students at Washington State University took part in the study. Analyses of data received from a twenty-one-item attitude inventory revealed positive change toward the course for sixteen items at or beyond the .05 level of significance. Of these sixteen items, thirteen were at or beyond the .001 level. The two items of greatest change were: "At first I felt that I wasn't getting anything from this course, but lately I've noticed myself observing behavior of other people and comparing them with what I've learned in class," and "I do not feel that in this course there has been enough attention given to feedback information for the students' benefit."

HARVEY, J. N., AND BARKER, D. G. "Student Evaluation of Teaching Effectiveness." *Improving College and University Teaching,* 1970, *18,* 275–278.

The author examined the relationship between students' gross subjective judgments and their responses to a typical rating scale. The basic data were collected from 118 male students. The ten items rated highest on a scale of twenty-one were: objectives clarified by the instructor, organization of course, knowledge of subject, range of interests and culture, preparation for class, skill as lecturer, skill as discussion leader, variety in classroom techniques, assignments, and ability to arouse interest.

HATCH, W. R., AND BENNET, A. "Effectiveness in Teaching." *New Dimensions in Higher Education.* Washington, D.C.: U.S. Department of Health, Education, and Welfare, 1965.

Studies in various areas of teacher effectiveness are outlined. The latest research on the effectiveness of teaching suggested that: the critical factor is not class size but the nature of teaching as it affects learning; one teaching method is no more effective than another; and problem-oriented approaches are becoming more effective.

HAYES, J. R. "Research, Teaching, and Faculty Fate." *Science,* 1971, *172,* 227–230.

Data were collected from 355 individuals in seventeen academic departments at Carnegie-Mellon University in the Colleges of Engineering and Science, Humanities and Social Sciences, and in the business and resource management department. The study provides evidence on three questions. (1) Are research activity and teaching ability related to each other? The answer is not wholly clear. If one takes department heads' judgments at face value, there is evidence of a strong positive relation between research ability and teaching quality. If one interprets the correlation in the department heads' judgments as a "halo" effect, then there is no evidence that research activity and teaching ability are related. (2) In what way do research activity and teaching ability influence classroom assignment? Individuals with high research ability and high rank tend to be assigned to high-level classes. Teaching quality is unrelated to classroom assignment, but there may be a tendency to give "bad" researchers greater teaching loads than "good" researchers. (3) In what way do research activity and teaching ability influence promotion? Promotion is strongly related to measures of research activity but appears to be unrelated to teaching ability.

HAYES, R. B. "A Way to Measure Classroom Teaching Effectiveness." *Journal of Teacher Education,* 1963, *14,* 168–176.

This study included 660 sophomores at The Pennsylvania State University who were taking a required course in the Reserve Officer Training Program. Its objective was to develop a satisfactory unidimensional instrument to measure student attitudes toward teaching effectiveness. An instrument of nine items measuring teaching effectiveness resulted. The study indicates that an unfavorable attitude toward a required course does not appear to affect appreciably the instructor ratings, for 70 percent of the students with unfavorable course attitudes rated their instructors above-average. (For further statistical data, see HAYES, R. B. "A Way to Measure Teaching." *The Journal of Educational Research,* 1963, *57,* 47–50.)

HEFFERLIN, J. B. *The Dynamics of Academic Reform.* San Francisco: Jossey-Bass, 1969.

HEILMAN, J. D., AND ARMENTROUT, W. D. "The Rating of College Teachers on Ten Traits by Their Students." *The Journal of Educational Psychology,* 1936, *27,* 197–216.

The results of this study were obtained from student ratings of teachers at the Colorado State College of Education over the period 1927–1930 and again in 1935. The PRSI was used throughout. These conclusions were drawn: students in any class vary widely in ratings given to an individual instructor, and also the teachers are rated very differently on each trait as well as on the scale as a whole. A group of twenty-three teachers which was rated during both periods showed a slight decrease in the later ratings. Ratings showed no reliable differences among the teachers who differed from five to twenty or more years in their teaching experience, and none among the ratings of groups who differed from five to thirty or more years in age. The factors of class size, severity of grading, the traits measured by the Bernreuter

Personality Inventory, the students' interest in the course, the sex of the teacher, and the maturity of the rater were not found to affect the ratings. The reliability of the Purdue Scale was about .75.

HESTER, J. D. In private correspondence, 1972.

HEXTER, J. H. "Publish or Perish—a Defense." *The Public Interest,* 1969, *17,* 60–77.

Hexter's defense for the "publish or perish" position, used the widely publicized Yale incident as focal point. "The advantage of Publish or Perish is that it breaks through two parochial and absurd assumptions: (1) that all university teaching goes on in the classroom, and (2) that in all teaching that goes on there is a pure act of creation on the part of the classroom teacher."

HEYNS, R. W. "Summary: Conference on Appraisal of Teaching in Large Universities." In W. J. McKeachie (Ed.), *The Appraisal of Teaching in Large Universities.* Ann Arbor, Mich.: The University of Michigan Extension Service, 1959.

Evaluation has its healthiest consequences when the procedures call attention to the processes of both teaching and learning. Teaching must be seen in terms of the total nature of the university and its unique function—that of research. Student ratings have principal value when they accurately reflect opinions on those matters on which students are most expert—their own reactions. Evaluation of teaching involves evaluation of changes in students, evaluation of changes in courses, and evaluation of changes in the entire program. In our search for new and better techniques, we should not refrain from improving present methods for assigning rewards such as peer judgments and decision processes within departments. We must be on guard that evaluation procedures do not arouse too much anxiety, decrease student sense of responsibility, take too much time, become ends in themselves, and serve as substitutes for making judgments.

HICKS, L. E. "Some Properties of Ipsative, Normative, and Forced-Choice Normative Measures." *Psychological Bulletin,* 1970, *74,* 167–184.

A review of relevant literature describing mathematical and empirical properties of ipsative and nonipsative measures (normative or forced-choice normative) was undertaken. The literature was evaluated and summarized, and the need for a simple procedure for quantifying the "degree of ipsativity" in measuring instruments was indicated. The paper concludes that although nonipsative measuring instruments can be highly effective in most assessment situations, purely ipsative instruments, on the other hand, possess such extensive psychometric limitations that their use is not recommended. (Each ipsative score for an individual is dependent on his own scores on other variables, but it is independent of, and not comparable with, the scores of other individuals.)

HIGHET, G. *The Art of Teaching.* New York: Alfred A. Knopf, 1950.

HILDEBRAND, M. "How to Recommend Promotion for a Mediocre Teacher Without Actually Lying." *Experiment and Innovation: New Directions in Education at the University of California,* 1971, *4,* 1–21. (This article appears in slightly altered form in *The Journal of Higher Education,* 1972, *43,* 44–62.

This article is presented as a narrative report of a "hypothetical" case involving the promotion of Dr. Blank. The author clinically analyzes the letters of recommendation and concludes that they are inadequate. He points out that an unfortunate consequence to the promotion of mediocre teachers is denial of promotion to some excellent teachers. The article also analyzes twenty-three objections of those who oppose the regular use of student evaluation of teaching. Some research findings from a University of California at Davis study of student evaluation of instruction also are included.

HILDEBRAND, M., AND OTHERS. *Evaluating University Teaching.* Berkeley, Calif.: Center for Research and Development in Higher Education, 1971.

This three-year study conducted at the University of California at Davis had two major aims: to define and describe effective teaching to help instructors improve and graduate students prepare for teaching; and to find more valid, reliable, and effective means of incorporating the evaluation of teaching into advancement procedures. The study involved more than 1,600 students and faculty members. Some of its principal findings are: Eighty-five items characterize "best" teachers as perceived by students and fifty-four items characterize them as perceived by colleagues; and all items statistically discriminate "best" from "worst" teachers with a high level of significance. Among *students,* the five components of effective teaching performance are an analytic/synthetic approach, organization/clarity, instructor-group interaction, instructor-individual student interaction, and dynamism/enthusiasm. Among *colleagues,* best teachers are marked by research activity and recognition, intellectual breadth, participation in the academic community, relations with students, concern for teaching. In general, student ratings of "best" teachers showed only negligible correlations with academic rank of instructor, class level, number of courses previously taken in the same department, class size, required versus optional course, course in major or not, sex of respondent, class level, grade-point average, and expected grade in course. There is excellent agreement among students, and between faculty and students, about the effectiveness of given teachers. "Best" and "worst" teachers engage in the same professional activities and allocate their time among academic pursuits in about the same ways, and the mere performance of activities associated with teaching does not ensure effective instruction. A disproportionate number of "best" teachers were teaching seminar rather than lecture courses, and a wide range of excellence was revealed in the teaching of different subject areas. Students evaluated the positive contributions made to their lives by "best" teachers in six areas: knowledge imparted, counsel given, objectives clarified, values developed, incentive elicited, and skills developed; and correlations of mean scores for these areas with mean scores for the components of effective teaching and with overall ratings of effectiveness of teaching are high. Nine types of effective teachers were identified by analyzing individual patterns of relatively high and low scores on the five components of effective teaching. Teachers rated as excellent by some observers and as poor by others are less consistent in their performance of the five components of effective teaching than are "best" teachers. (For other results of the study, see Wilson and others, 1969.)

HILDEBRAND, M., AND WILSON, R. D. "Report to the Faculty on the Effective University Teaching and Its Evaluation." In K. G. Eble (Ed.), *The Recognition and Evaluation of Teaching*. Salt Lake City: Project to Improve College Teaching and the Committee on Evaluation, 1971.

HILGERT, R. L. "Teacher or Researcher?" *The Educational Forum*, 1964, *28*, 463–468.

Those who favor teaching argue the following points: (1) degree, research, or publication do not guarantee that one will be an effective teacher; (2) knowledge of the subject is secondary to the ability to impart knowledge to the student; and (3) promotions and salary increases should be based first of all on the professor's competence as a teacher.

Those who favor research and writing offer the following arguments: (1) research and writing reinforce the teaching efforts; (2) students consider the professor's knowledge to be authoritative when he has published a substantial amount; (3) research and writing are modes of preparation for classroom presentation; (4) research updates teaching; and (5) professors should speak out in today's troubled world. The answer to the problem remains a matter of individual choice.

HILLWAY, T. "Evaluating College and University Administration."
Intellect, 1973, *101*, 426–427.

The author writes that in view of the "burgeoning influence" of administration on the educational program and in light of recent public demands for accountability, attempts to evaluate the work of administrators more carefully and fairly are in order. A rating scale of fifteen qualities and nine methods or activities has been developed. Desirable qualities are: interest in the progress of education, educational and cultural background, sympathetic attitude toward students, fairness in dealing with students, considerate attitude toward faculty, self-adjustment and sense of humor, tolerance of new ideas, trustworthiness (honesty and reliability), skill in securing group action, ability to inspire confidence, ability to organize, ability to maintain faculty morale, ability to maintain faculty performance, and appearance (dress and grooming). Methods are: encourages democratic participation, communicates effectively with group members, presents appropriate materials for group action, adheres faithfully to group decisions, respects professional rights of faculty, assigns work fairly and suitably, makes fair decisions on promotions and salary, makes contributions to his academic field, and uses appropriate administrative methods.

HIND, R. R. "Analysis of a Faculty: Professionalism, Evaluation, and the Authority Structure." In J. V. Baldridge (Ed.), *Academic Governance*. Berkeley, Calif.: McCutchan Publishing, 1971.

The study was made during the 1967–1968 academic year with a stratified (by rank) random sample of 100 faculty members of the School of Humanities and Sciences at Stanford University. The study found that 53 percent of total professional time was devoted to all kinds of teaching, primarily undergraduate and graduate; 32 percent to research and scholarship; 11 percent to university service; and 4 percent to external service. When asked about the influence of each task in determining university rewards, research and teaching were ranked in that order; and when asked about which tasks should determine university rewards, research maintained top rating but with markedly reduced differential. Overall satisfaction with the evaluation process was high, with 49 percent responding "extremely" or "very satisfied," 40 percent "moderately satisfied," and 11 percent "slightly" or "not at all satisfied." When asked about perceived influence of evaluators of teaching, "extremely and very influential" and "moderately influential" ratings were given as follows: department head (47); department colleagues (46); students (36); dean (12); outsiders (8); other faculty (5); provost and above (4); and appointments and promotions committee (3). When asked about perceived influence of evaluators of research, the responses were: department colleagues (73); department head (66); faculty at other institutions (62); dean (29); provost (12); appointments and promotions committee (12); grant makers (11); other faculty (11); other outsiders (6); president and trustees (3); and students (1). There seems to be sufficient evidence of success to urge that systematic student evaluation procedures be established and supported by university administrations, both for constructive feedback to individual teachers and as a positive way of increasing the influence of teaching in the evaluation-reward system.

HODGKINSON, H. L. "How to Evaluate Faculty When You Don't Know Much About Them." *The Research Reporter* (The Center for Research and Development in Higher Education), 1972, 7, 5–8.

The author contends that the central purpose of evaluation should be to assist an individual (student or a teacher) to improve his performance, but most evaluation systems work primarily to reject people rather than to help them. The assessment must be available continuously when the individual believes he or she needs it. He should also be encouraged and assisted to develop his own criteria for increasing his competence and understanding of the assessment feedback in terms of his own goals. At the faculty level, the system should encourage collaboration between colleagues in order to improve teaching rather than set them against each other. Any system which attempts to assess and reward teaching competence must be highly flexible and individualistic. The uniform approach to defining teaching competence is perhaps at the heart of the issue. Few institutions are turning to "growth contracts" for faculty members, and even for those on tenure the growth contract indicates that faculty members are expected to grow and will be assisted in doing so. Hodgkinson also discusses classroom visitation by colleagues and the use of video tapes for teaching improvement.

HODGKINSON, H. L. "Assessment and Reward Systems." In G. K. Smith (Ed.), *New Teaching New Learning.* San Francisco: Jossey-Bass, 1971.

The reward structure has two general strategies: The first is simply to increase rewards for those jobs that must be performed at the highest level of competence. The second is to decrease the level of threat in those jobs so that people will move into new tasks with a greater feeling of security and well-being. Evaluation should exist for the central purpose of helping students and teachers improve performance. Most evaluation systems, however, work primarily to reject people rather than to help them improve. Concise criteria would be helpful, but the criteria used for students and for faculty promotion are usually ambiguous and do not allow much individuality, which is important in both teaching and learning.

The assessment must continuously be available for teacher or student, so that the individual may benefit from it whenever he thinks he needs it. The system should make maximum feedback on performance available constantly. In order that the feedback does not have to be labeled in an evaluative way except on a person's past performance, any reward system should be based on intrinsic motivations rather than on extrinsic ones. The author recommends the contract system in which the incoming person is asked to state as clearly as possible the goals he hopes to attain during his period of residence. The institutional representative then states how the institution is prepared to commit itself to help him attain his objectives. In addition to the contract system, universities endorse the direct observation of classroom teaching by one's colleagues. If teaching is an important professional criterion for promotion within an institution, such decisions are less than professional unless other professionals are in the room watching the teacher teach.

HOLMES, D. S. "The Relationship Between Expected Grades and Students' Evaluations of Their Instructors." *Educational and Psychological Measurement* (in press).

Seven lecture classes in the College of Arts and Sciences at the University of Texas, each with an enrollment over 100, were evaluated. The responses of students expecting A's (200), B's (752), and C's (587) were compared on each of eighteen evaluative items. Data from students who expected grades of D or F were not considered because they constituted fewer than 7 percent of the students. It was found that students who had expected lower grades reported less personal involvement in the course than did students expecting higher grades but, contrary to what was expected, those anticipating lower grades were not more critical of the instructors' presentations than were students expecting higher grades. Thus it did not appear that expected grades were related to a general halo effect.

HOLMES, D. S. "The Teaching Assessment Blank: A Form for the Student Assessment of College Instructors." *The Journal of Experimental Education*, 1971, *39*, 34–38.

A factor analysis based on evaluations filled out by 1,648 students at the University of Texas revealed four evaluative factors which measured (1) the quality of the instructors' presentations, (2) the evaluation process and the student-instructor interactions, (3) the degree to which the students were stimulated and motivated by the instructors, and (4) the clarity of the tests. A further analysis indicated that sub-scale scores reflecting the factor scores could be developed from the total item pool. Of particular interest is the identification of the student stimulation factor. The degree to which instructors instill interest, enthusiasm, and motivation is an important aspect to measure.

HOLMES, D. S. *The Effects of Disconfirmed Grade Expectancies on Students' Evaluations of Their Instructor: A Study of Attitude Change.* Unpublished document. Princeton, N.J.: Educational Testing Service, 1970.

At the University of Texas, half the students who deserved and expected A's and B's were given their expected grades while half were given a grade that was one step lower than they had expected. After receiving their grades, the students filled out the teaching assessment form used there. A two-by-two analysis of variance revealed no differences in evaluations as a function of differences in grades, but evaluations on eleven of the nineteen items were lowered as a function of the unexpected lowering of grades. It was concluded that although differences in actual grades do not affect evaluations, if students' grades disconfirm their expectancies, the students will tend to depreciate the instructor's performance in areas other than his grading system.

HUDELSON, E. "The Validity of Student Rating of Instructors." *School and Society,* 1951, *73,* 265–266.

This study done at West Virginia University sought to determine whether students rated instructors according to the marks those instructors gave them. The coefficient of correlation between marks and ratings was .19. The author concluded that these students could not fairly be charged with letting marks influence their opinions of their instructors as teachers.

HUMPHREY, D. C., AND MC CREARY, E. C. "Evaluating the Teaching of History." *Liberal Education,* 1970, *56,* 519–531.

After surveying over one hundred history departments, it was found that many colleges either ignored teacher evaluation or found it an insurmountable task. Based upon this finding, the authors (in the history department at Carnegie-Mellon University) developed a system of evaluation for history. Their statement of "criteria for good teaching" consists of two parts: a discussion of criteria for substantive goals in history courses, and a discussion of four important conditions of learning (motivation, high standards of performance, structure, and guidance). The essay concludes with examinations of self- and student evaluation.

HUNTER, J. O. "Faculty Evaluations as a Liberal Persuasion." *Improving College and University Teaching*, 1969, *17*, 90–92.

The author contends that in developing any system of evaluation, decisiveness is less important than good faith. Especially in the community college still seeking its identity, a collegial spirit should obviate coercive methods. Seen in this light, evaluation is a matter for persuasion which emanates from a liberal base. The teacher expects that the system shall be enlightening and instructive rather than merely laudatory or abrasively critical. Four instruments for evaluation are suggested: student ratings, classroom visitation, a colleague relationship (senior and junior professor) on teaching, and an evaluation portfolio.

HUTCHINSON, W. R. "Yes, John, There Are Teachers on the Faculty." *American Scholar*, 1966, *35*, 430–441.

The article is in response to another by Fischer in *Harper's* (also abstracted). "If there is an award this year for the slogan that has most confused the public dialogue, 'publish or perish' should be in the running. . . . Inferior teaching is not going to be corrected by diagnoses that are even more inferior; and the antiresearch diagnosis applies remotely if at all, in the case of 95 percent of our institutions. . . . The fact is that no very vital instruction of any kind can be carried on without scholarly books and the studies and monographs that undergird them." The author quotes Pearson of Bennington College (he has had thirty years of experience with student ratings) : "The overwhelming evidence is that those faculty members who rate highest with the students are the most productive scholars in their field. There are exceptions of course, but there is no doubt whatever of the predominant tendency."

HYMAN, S. C. "The Teacher as Scholar: Ersatz Image?" *The Chronicle of Higher Education,* Jan. 8, 1973.

The author contends that no single dogma is more central to the accepted philosophy of higher education than is the notion that a university faculty member must be a scholar as well as a teacher. That concept shapes the university's structure; it controls the way we select our faculties, how we reward them, apportion their responsibilities, and what we expect of them. When a faculty member does not have a commitment to scholarly research, it should be possible for one to see his lifelong progress and career advancement stemming from relationships to students and teaching. In moving toward implementation, there may be a vastly expanded role for the independent research institute and the so-called "think tanks" that have been developing. "We must redefine scholarship to be the primary responsibility of a relative few and . . . teaching must be the primary responsibility of the many on the university faculty."

"Improving College Teaching." *School and Society,* 1968, *95,* 271–272.

A helpful program at the University of Colorado's School of Education provides professors with an opportunity to meet with Homer C. Rainey, professor emeritus of higher education. He meets with one or two teachers a day to discuss their particular teaching problems. A monthly seminar is provided to facilitate discussion in this area.

INGRAHAM, M. H. "Administrative Implications and Problems." In

W. J. McKeachie (Ed.), *The Appraisal of Teaching in Large Universities.* Ann Arbor, Mich.: The University of Michigan Extension Service, 1959.

The author suggests that the relationship between good research and good teaching is highly correlated and nonlinear. A poor researcher will be a poor teacher, one who is stultified; and someone who devotes too much time to research will also be a poor teacher, lacking sufficient interest in teaching. The constancy and quality of research is more important than the quantity. Evaluation of research is not easy but it should be the major task of the administrator. The author would promote the good researcher over the good teacher, for the university's fate is tied with scholarship. Teacher evaluation is important for the light it sheds on the teaching process and for the help it gives instructors but is less important for administrative purposes. The administrator will generally find out who are the successful teachers.

Institute for Higher Education. *Student Evaluation of Teaching: Presentations at a Conference.* Pittsburgh, Pa.: University of Pittsburgh, 1970.

Two papers are included in this report. One by W. J. McKeachie, "Research on Student Ratings of Teaching," discusses his AAUP article on evaluation of teaching and, particularly, criticisms of it. He cautions that student evaluation of teaching can be valid but the ultimate purpose of evaluating teaching is to improve learning. Evaluation is not an end in itself. A second paper by George L. Fahey, "Student Rating of Teaching: Some Questionable Assumptions," concludes that student rating procedures are probably more objective, reliable, and perhaps more valid than is any alternative procedure we now use for such assessment. The ratings procedures however, should be carefully interpreted.

ISAACSON, R. L., AND OTHERS. "Dimensions of Student Evaluations of Teaching." *Journal of Educational Psychology,* 1964, *55,* 344–351.

Two groups of students in introductory psychology (1260 in all) rated their teachers on a 46-item questionnaire. Six factors appeared which were consistent: skill, overload (difficulty factor), structure, feedback, group interaction, and student-teacher rapport.

ISAACSON, R. L., AND OTHERS. "Correlation of Teacher Personality Variables and Student Ratings." *Journal of Educational Psychology*, 1963, *54*, 110–117.

Relevant traits to teaching generally include five personality factors—surgency, agreeableness, dependability, emotional stability, and culture. The purpose of this study was to determine whether these personality traits can correlate with effective college teaching. The only high correlation achieved (0.48) was between the peer rating of culture and student ratings of effectiveness.

JOHNSON, J. A. "Instruction: From the Consumer's View." In C. B. T. Lee (Ed.), *Improving College Teaching*. Washington, D.C.: American Council on Education, 1967.

JOHNSTONE, J. W. C., AND RIVERA, R. J. *Volunteers for Learning: A Study of the Educational Pursuits of American Adults.* Chicago: Aldine Publishing Co., 1965.

KARMAN, T. A. "Faculty Evaluation." *Liberal Education,* 1969, *55*, 539–544.

A new faculty evaluation system developed for Defiance College incorporates three decision-making levels on faculty performance—the dean, division chairman, and the students. In the spring, the division chairman and the dean submit progress reports evaluating each teacher in seven areas: classroom effectiveness, student relations in general, constructivity regarding college programs, ability to work with other faculty members, committee effectiveness, administrative effectiveness, and community relations. (Not all categories apply to each person.) The students use a five-point scale for judging teaching effectiveness. Strengths and weaknesses and a plan for dealing with the latter are developed for each instructor.

KELLER, R. J., AND DOBBIN, J. E. "Faculty Promotion Policies and Practices." In R. E. Eckert and R. J. Keller (Eds.), *A University Looks at Its Program.* Minneapolis: University of Minnesota Press, 1954.

The dignity and prestige of a state university as well as that of any college depend on the faculty. Based upon a survey of promotion policies at other educational institutions, the authors conclude that most actually place little emphasis on teaching ability as a factor in promoting staff members. A further survey was undertaken of all 105 University of Minnesota deans and department heads, with 35 responses. The variations in practice from department to department were found to be so great, and the interrelationships of factors so complex, that no general pattern of standards or procedures could be derived from the results. The administrators who took part in this survey provided ample evidence that a staff member's promotion or nonpromotion was largely an individual matter, contingent upon one or more factors that may vary from time to time.

KENNEDY, W. R. "The Relationship of Selected Student Characteristics to Components of Teacher/Course Evaluations Among Freshmen English Students at Kent State University." Research paper presented at Annual Meeting of the American Education Research Association, 1972. Chicago, Ill.

The objective of this study was to determine the relationships between student ratings on the components of a teacher /course evaluation instrument and their scores on selected Omnibus Personality Inventory subscales, American College Test (ACT) scores, "expected grade," "actual grade," "expected-actual grade" differential in the course, grade-point average, and the variables of sex and college membership. The subjects were 549 freshmen English students. Some of the findings: of the twenty ACT correlations, none were significant, indicating that students' teacher and course evaluations were independent of ability as measured by ACT scores; students with higher grade-point averages (A and B) rated the instructor significantly higher than did students with low grade-point averages (C and D).

KENT, L. "Student Evaluation of Teaching." *The Educational Record,* 1966, *47,* 376–406.

In only one institution in ten are systematic student ratings used in all or most departments, the American Council on Education Survey of 1966 found. Such ratings are not used at all in 48 percent of the institutions surveyed. Those who have seriously examined the question of student evaluation feel that students are very perceptive and that ratings are not affected by such factors as rater's or teacher's sex, class size, or grade-point average. Students do tend to be overly lenient in their ratings, particularly in cases where the administration conducts the program and requires evaluation of all its faculty members.

KERLINGER, F. N. "Student Evaluation of University Professors." *School and Society,* October 1971, *99,* 353–356.

An analysis of student evaluations of professors and their teaching determined that such evaluations are not an integral part of the instructional process and thus alienate professors. As a result they cause instructor hostility and resentment, undermine professional autonomy, diminish professional motivation, and erode professional responsibility. The article supports responsible evaluation of instruction—that which is initiated and conducted by professors as part of instruction.

KILLIAN, J. R. "Teaching Is Better Than Ever." *Atlantic,* 1965, *216,* 53–56.

The author speaks to the critics who fan the "publish or perish" fires, contending that "neglect of teaching" or "flight from teaching" have become contagious cliches that glibly convey a one-sided view of university teaching. "There is much on the other side, and it is important to highlight the good if we are to pinpoint the bad. On balance, I firmly believe that the good heavily outweighs the bad, that the present emphasis on research in our universities has had the result in most places of improving the quality of teaching. . . . Teachers who do no research or who fail to deepen their mastery of their fields are likely to become teachers of obsolete knowledge."

KINDALL, A. F., AND GATZA, J. "Positive Program for Performance Appraisal." *Harvard Business Review*, 1963, *41*, 153–154+.

KIRCHNER, R. P. "A Control Factor in Teacher Evaluation by Students." Unpublished research paper. Lexington, Ky.: College of Education, University of Kentucky, 1969.

The purpose of this research study was to determine whether the individual administering an evaluation instrument has any significant effect on the results, and which evaluation is most representative of the students' real evaluation of the teacher. This study, involving ten sections and 227 students in an introductory educational psychology course, found a significant difference (at .05 level) between whether or not the instructor or a neutral individual administered the student evaluation form. Higher ratings were achieved when the instructor administered the survey.

KOSSOFF, E. "Evaluating College Professors by 'Scientific' Methods." *The American Scholar*, 1971–1972, *41*, 79–93.

The author criticizes the mechanistic and the alleged pseudoscientific nature of evaluation instruments. "Only human thought can provide answers to the problems of evaluation. Human beings—not questionnaires, not evaluation instruments, not computers—produce evaluations. I have no objections to evaluation of teachers by human observers. Criticism of humans by humans I consider fair play. I object only to evaluation of humans by 'instruments' and 'mechanisms' to which are attributed superhuman powers of perception, precision, and perspicacity."

LADD, E. C., AND LIPSET, S. M. "Politics of Academic Natural Scientists and Engineers." *Science*, 1972, *176*, 1091–1100.

LANGEN, T. D. F. "Student Assessment of Teaching Effectiveness." *Improving College and University Teaching*, 1966, *14*, 22–25.

At the University of Washington 43 years of assessing student opinion of teaching resulted in a ten-item survey form. Analysis indicates that there is no relationship between the rating received by the instructor and the grade the student expects to receive from the course. A system of rating has merit, but the same items should not be used for all disciplines and for all levels of instruction.

LAURITS, J. "Thoughts on the Evaluation of Teaching." *The Evaluation of Teaching*. Washington, D.C.: Pi Lambda Theta, 1967. Betty J. Humphry, colloquy moderator.

The author discusses some problems associated with evaluation at various levels. He explains that the school has a responsibility to the student. The main burden of the evaluation of teaching must rest with the teachers—the process should become a part of the teaching process itself. Model schools or pilot institutions can be designated to study evaluation methods and procedures.

LEE, C. B. T. (Ed.) *Improving College Teaching*. Washington, D.C.: American Council on Education, 1967. 407 pp.

This important book centers around and comments on eight papers prepared for the American Council on Education. The work is essential for those interested in evaluation, particularly Part 4 on "Teaching and Learning" and Part 5 on "The Evaluation of Teaching Performance."

LEHMANN, I. J. "Evaluation of Instruction." In P. L. Dressel and

Associates, *Evaluation in Higher Education*. Boston: Houghton Mifflin, 1961.

The author contends that it is necessary to specify the functions of instruction before evaluation can take place. These functions, in sequential order, are: motivate the student, demonstrate to the student just what is expected of him, select appropriate practice tasks which are extensive and meaningful, provide the student with some satisfaction in his progress, organize the material so the cumulative significance of learning is readily apparent to the student, and provide the learner with high standards of performance and means for judging his performance. Several types of rating scales are presented and discussed: descriptive, numerical, graphic, forced-choice, or man-to-man; and several methods for evaluating instruction also are presented and discussed: peer ratings, student ratings, and course ratings. Because of the elusive nature of the teaching-learning process, no completely adequate mode of evaluation exists, but there is evidence that properly constructed rating scales are valuable, especially when the emphasis is placed on improvement of the quality of instruction.

The items composing the scales consisted primarily of behaviors observed by students in the classroom setting. But since faculty members often do not have an opportunity to observe colleagues' behavior in the classroom, information yielded by Colleague Teacher-Description Scales may be a useful supplement to information derived from students' observations. Taken together, the two sources of information comprise a more comprehensive definition of the roles and behavior of effective teachers.

LEWIS, E. C. "An Investigation of Student-Teacher Interaction as a Determiner of Effective Teaching." *Journal of Educational Research*, 1964, 57, 360–363.

The purpose of the investigation was to determine whether students and teachers tend to interact along measurable personality dimensions. Three groups of students were chosen: the first two groups provided a control of sex (male) and variation of subject matter, while the third group provided a variation of sex. Each student, as well as selected instructors in various fields, completed two questionnaires—The Guilford-Zimmerman Temperament Survey, and a one hundred-item biographical inventory. The results did not support the hypothesis. It was also concluded that effective teachers cannot be differentiated from less effective teachers on the basis of personality variables.

LOCKSLEY, N. "A Mathematical Look at Evaluation of Teaching." *School Science and Mathematics*, 1967, *67*, 797–798.

An experiment was undertaken to see how difficult it would be to mathematically develop some exact measure of teaching performance. What the observer hopes he is evaluating —teaching performance—is actually the sum of teaching ability, environmental influence on teaching, bias toward the person, bias toward the field, and two random errors—errors in teaching performance and errors in observation. The author concludes that the problems of evaluation seem too complex for mathematical measurement.

LOVELL, G. C., AND HANER, C. F. "Forced-Choice Applied to College Faculty Rating." *Educational and Psychological Measurement*, 1955, *15*, 291–304.

This study was concerned with the construction of a forced-choice type of rating scale to measure student evaluation of teachers and with items considered by students as important characteristics of faculty members. It was based on essays written by 100 Grinnell College seniors describing their "best" and "worst" college teachers. Faculty and students were in good agreement as to items describing best, average, and worst professors, and in very close agreement as to those that differentiate between best and worst. The study also found: lower ratings for instructors teaching larger classes (thirty-one and up) with significance at the 1 percent level of confidence; instructors teaching required courses received significantly lower ratings than did those teaching nonrequired ones; comparison of differences in ratings of male and female students was not significant; and differences between seniors and each of the other three classes was significant at the 1 percent or 2 percent level, but differences between other classes were not significant. A chief claim of the forced-choice type of rating scale is that it reduces deliberate faking of scores by students who wish to assign a high or low rating to a teacher regardless of objectivity.

LUNDSTEDT, s. "Criteria for Effective Teaching." *Improving College and University Teaching,* 1966, *14,* 27–31.

The article focuses on the point that teaching is basically communication. Criteria essential to good teaching and related to communication are: knowledge of one's subject matter, empathy, and sense of timing. Proper timing is the most difficult to achieve in class. The effective communicator is generally the effective teacher.

MANN, w. R. "Changes in the Level of Attitude Sophistication of College Students as a Measure of Teacher Effectiveness." *Dissertation Abstracts,* 1969, *29* (8-A), 2443(A)-2444(A).

The study examines the instructor's behavior in the classroom and the personality and achievement characteristics of college students as possible variables to explain changes in attitude sophistication. The research design included an experimental group of 286 students in an introductory economics course and a control group of thirty-one history students. The major findings were: since the experimental group increased in attitude sophistication more than did the control group, course content and instructors do make a difference; the course grade was positively related to achiever personality, the students' SAT mathematics score, a test of economic understanding taken before the course began, a reading accuracy test, and general teaching skill; attitude sophistication was positively related to social science interest, the students' SAT verbal score, student-teacher rapport, and change in beliefs; and attitude sophistication and the course grade are determined by different sets of instructor and student variables.

MARTIN, T. W., AND BERRY, K. J. "The Teaching-Research Dilemma: Its Sources in the University Setting." *The Journal of Higher Education,* 1969, *40,* 691–703.

Professors are caught in the dilemma of an interpositional role conflict: teach for the university or publish for the profession. The university hires a professor mainly to teach but retains or promotes him largely on the basis of his scholarship. The authors advocate a separation of research and teaching functions as a way of resolving the inherent role conflict.

MASLOW, A. H., AND ZIMMERMAN, W. "College Teaching Ability, Scholarly Activity and Personality." *The Journal of Educational Psychology,* 1956, *47,* 185–189.

Research carried out at Brooklyn College over a three-year period, 1943–1946 asked: "Is creativeness (research activity in the field, writing) in a college teacher positively or negatively correlated with goodness of teaching?" Data were collected on eighty-six teachers. It was concluded that, at least at the Brooklyn College, colleagues tend to equate good teaching with creativeness (.77) and students tend to equate good teaching with good personality (.76). Also, students and faculty agree fairly well on who the good teachers are (.69), but their concept of personality is quite different. The faculty concept of personality is relatively independent of all of the other rated traits.

MAYHEW, L. B. "A Tissue Committee for Teachers." *Improving College and University Teaching,* 1967, *15,* 5–10.

College teaching seems to have exempted itself from any kind of realistic assessment, in contrast to most other professions, which have developed means of evaluation (for example, a pathological tissue committee in medicine). Sequentially, the evaluation process consists of formulating broad educational purposes or objectives, specifying them into discrete behavorial terms, seeking appropriate relevant learning experiences, accumulating evidence of successful or unsuccessful demonstration of desired behaviors, and, finally, making judgments as to whether or not the broad educational objectives have been achieved.

The four reasonable sources for evidence about teaching effectiveness are the teacher himself, the student, someone who has seen teaching in progress, and demonstrations of behaviors which the teaching was intended to modify.

MC DANIEL, E. D., AND FELDHUSEN, J. F. "Relationships Between Faculty Ratings and Indexes of Service and Scholarship." *Proceedings of the 78th Annual Convention of the American Psychological Association,* 1970, *5,* 619–620.

Using a sample of seventy-six professors and 4,484 students at Purdue University, the authors found that the most effective instructors are those who write no books and those who limit their roles as paper and article writers to second authorship. Findings indicate no relationship between research activity, as indicated by grants, and instructional effectiveness. Time spent counseling students or supervising laboratories is positively related to instructional effectiveness, while time spent lecturing or in administration is negatively related to instructional effectiveness. With respect to class size, the results clearly indicate that the larger the class the lower are the ratings of instructional effectiveness.

MC DONOGH, E. C. "Let's Grade the Professors," *AAUP Bulletin,* 1944, *30,* 83–86.

Every professor should be graded by his students in much the same manner that he grades them. The author proposes that upon completion of a course each student should turn in his evaluation of the teaching to the registrar's office. The registrar could strike an average from all student grades for a particular course, and this average grade would become the teaching mark of the professor. The grading of professors would place teaching in an important achievement category and would afford recognition and status to the deserving instructor.

MC GRATH, E. J. "Characteristics of Outstanding College Teachers." *The Journal of Higher Education* 1962, *33*, 148–152.

A questionnaire survey was made of seventy-five teachers in fourteen liberal arts colleges that were judged by an administrative officer to be unusually good. These individuals held different views regarding the contribution that a life of continued research activity makes to effective undergraduate teaching. A majority, especially among the natural scientists, believed that research done by the teacher of undergraduates improves his teaching ability. If, however, research were limited to original investigation, and did not include the imaginative combining of existing facts into new generalizations or the interpretation of factual data, the percentage of those who considered it essential to good undergraduate teaching would fall considerably. The view seems substantiated that scholarship is a sine qua non of vital and stimulating teaching but that in some fields original investigation is a doubtful requirement for all teachers.

MC GUIRE, C. "A Proposed Model for the Evaluation of Teaching." In *The Evaluation of Teaching*. Washington, D.C.: Pi Lambda Theta, 1967. Betty J. Humphry, colloquy moderator.

The author's model includes three dimensions or axes: inputs—teachers, students, setting, materials, methods, costs, and goals sacrificed; outcomes—individual satisfactions, cognitive achievement, affective changes, and psychomotor achievement; and sources of information about the achievement of outcomes—expert opinion, participant reaction (student and teacher) observation, and performance (outcomes).

MC KEACHIE, W. J. "Research on Student Ratings of Teaching." In Alex J. Ducanis (Ed.), *Student Evaluation of Teaching.* Pittsburgh, Pa.: Institute for Higher Education, University of Pittsburgh, 1970.

The paper begins with some reactions to criticisms of the author's AAUP paper by Borgatta. (Both the AAUP paper and Borgatta's reactions are included in this bibliography.) McKeachie contends that student evaluation of teaching can be valid and useful, but the ultimate purpose of evaluating teaching is to improve learning. Evaluation is not an end in itself, and we must weigh the cost of evaluation against the gains. The college is a learning community, and evaluation of either students or teachers should be forced to justify its existence in terms of learning. He feels that evaluation of teaching in the future will be more explicit with respect to the teacher's effectiveness in achieving different objectives. If these objectives are specified students will discriminate between the different objectives. They may, for example, rate one teacher as effective in stimulating interest in continued learning but not effective in communicating knowledge, while another teacher may be effective in other respects. When these discriminations are made in research it may be found that the student, faculty, and objective measures of learning are more highly correlated than has been revealed by past research.

MC KEACHIE, W. J. "Student Ratings of Faculty." *AAUP Bulletin,* 1969, *55,* 439–444.

Increased interest in college teaching seems to be reflected in increased demands for ways of evaluating teaching. In spite of the somewhat spotty evidence on the validity of student evaluations of teaching, their use is increasing. That "feedback" or "knowledge of results" aids learning is a psychological principle of long standing. Used with other "feedback" devices, student evaluations may be of much value to teachers. (The article also includes a form for student evaluation of teaching.)

MC KEACHIE, W. J. "Appraising Teaching Effectiveness." In W. J. McKeachie (Ed.), *The Appraisal of Teaching in Large Universities.* Ann Arbor, Mich.: The University of Michigan Extension Service, 1959.

Four gaps in knowledge about teaching effectiveness are considered: we do not know very much about what college teachers do; we do not know how validly students can rate teaching effectiveness; we do know the relationship of teacher behavior to student learning; and we measure only a limited portion of our educational objectives by our traditional final examinations. To learn more about these issues, thirty instructors were observed in three large classes—elementary psychology, college algebra, and second-year French. Pairs of observers visited each class three times during the term, and items they observed were also asked of the students at the end of the term. These generalizations developed: teaching methods differed from course to course; while the results were not convincing, the author believed that students could rate instructor behaviors with relative accuracy; with respect to instructor effectiveness, there was little resemblance between the most successful teachers of French and the most successful teachers of psychology.

MC KEACHIE, W. J. AND SOLOMON, D. "Student Ratings of Instructors: A Validity Study." *Journal of Educational Research,* 1958, *51,* 379–382.

The study, which attempted to validate student ratings of instructors against the percentage of their students who elected advanced courses, was based upon the thesis that one criterion of an effective teacher would be his ability to arouse interest in his subject matter. In two of the five semesters, instructor ratings were significantly correlated with the percentage of continuing students; but on the whole the data did not indicate a very consistent relationship between student ratings and student interest as evidenced by election of advanced courses.

MC KEACHIE, W. J. "A Program for Training Teachers of Psychology." *The American Psychologist*, 1951, *6*, 119–121.

> The report describes an experimental program for training teachers of psychology at the University of Michigan. Also reported is the practice of having students rate the entire college faculty on the same scale (A, B, C, D, E) on which students are graded. Average ratings for the teaching fellows in psychology in their first term of teaching was 2.92, with A as 4, and so forth. In the second term it was 3.22, as compared with a 3.0 rating for all teachers in the college. This may be the answer to the occasional criticism of the use of graduate students as teachers.

MC KEACHIE, W. J., AND OTHERS. "Student Ratings of Teacher Effectiveness: Validity Studies." *American Educational Research Journal*, 1971, *8*, 435–445.

> The validity of student ratings of teaching effectiveness was assessed in five studies. Ratings of teachers on the "skill" factor were positively related to mean achievement in four of the five studies but not as consistently for men as for women. Women teachers rated high in "structure" were more effective than were men. Teachers rated high on "rapport" were effective on measures of student thinking. Teachers rated as having an impact on beliefs were effective in changing attitudes.

MC NEIL, J. D. "Concomitants of Using Behavioral Objectives in the Assessment of Teacher Effectiveness." *The Journal of Experimental Education*, 1967, *36*, 69–74.

> The author contends that data provide evidence that the emphasis and use of operational definitions of instructional goals, including specification of criterion measures in the supervisory process, is accompanied by more favorable assessment of teachers by supervisors and greater gain in desired directions on the part of learners.

MEAD EDUCATIONAL SERVICES. *The Seat of Heat: The Big City Superintendency.* Atlanta: Mead Educational Services, 1970.

MEDLEY, D. M., AND MITZEL, H. E. "Measuring Classroom Behavior by Systematic Observation." In N. L. Gage (Ed.), *Handbook of Research on Teaching.* Chicago: Rand McNally, 1963.

To learn something about the teaching process and its relationship to pupil learning appears to be the proper role of direct observation in research on teacher effectiveness. The main purpose of this section in the American Educational Research Association *Handbook* is to extract from a number of studies whatever can be learned that would be useful in planning future observational studies.

MEGAW, N. "The Dynamics of Evaluation." In C. B. T. Lee (Ed.), *Improving College Teaching.* Washington, D.C.: American Council on Education, 1967.

This work contains opinions on the advantages and disadvantages of evaluating teaching effectiveness. The present methods of objective evaluation are regarded as so ineffective that the only solution may well be completely subjective evaluation by a committee.

MEREDITH, G. M. "Dimensions of Faculty-Course Evaluation." *Journal of Psychobiology,* 1969, *73*, 27–32.

The study focuses on the dimensionality of faculty-course evaluation. The Illinois Course Evaluation Questionnaire and A Student's Rating Scale of an Instructor were administered to 1,097 students at the University of Hawaii. Sixty-seven variables were intercorrelated and factor analyzed, resulting in a nine-factor solution. The nine factors were: instructional impact, instructor impact, difficulty level, attention value, satisfaction with instructional method, instructor commitment, appropriate evaluation, and two other factors which were unlabeled because of their small percent of the rotated variance. The first two factors accounted for 64 percent of the rotated variance.

MEYER, P. R., AND PATTON, R. M. "Can Student Rating of Instructors Be Painless and Foolproof?" *School and Society,* 1954, *80,* 200–201.

Student ratings are likely to be careless, too general, biased, or unpalatable—more the fault of the instruments used than the students. To correct this deficiency, a forced-choice instrument was developed and tried with 208 students at two universities. The forced-choice scale discriminated between good and poor teachers very effectively. The "best" and "worst" groups constituted distinct distributions with little overlap. Based upon results when data on student faking was sought, the forced-choice scale was more foolproof than were any of the graphic or checklist types. The scale also discriminates between good-sounding teaching techniques which students find helpful and equally favorable-sounding practices which they consider of little importance.

MILLER, M. T. "Instructor Attitudes Toward, and Their Use of, Student Ratings of Teachers." *Journal of Educational Psychology,* 1971, *62,* 235–239.

The purpose of this study was to determine empirically whether providing instructors with information from student ratings effected their subsequent ratings by students and on student achievement, and whether these effects were a function of instructor attitudes toward the value of the student ratings. Thirty-six teaching assistants in three freshman courses at the University of Iowa were assigned to groups on the basis of an attitude scale regarding the value they ascribed to student ratings. Instructors in feedback or attitude groups did not differ significantly on their end-of-semester ratings by students from those who did not have access to the ratings; there were nonsignificant differences between instructor final ratings as a function of their attitudes toward the value of the ratings; and for the instructors in two of the three courses, feedback from students' ratings did not improve instruction and hence the academic performance of the students. A partial explanation for some findings might lie in lack of career teaching commitment on the part of some teaching assistants and hence a lack of motivation to use feedback data to improve instruction.

MILLER, R. I. *Evaluating Faculty Performance.* San Francisco: Jossey-Bass, 1972.

This first book-length treatment of faculty evaluation provides an overall system for faculty evaluation, which the author stresses should be adapted and not adopted. Nine areas for faculty evaluation are proposed: advising, classroom teaching, faculty service and relations, administration, performing and visual arts, professional status and activities, publications, public service, and research. Special attention is given to classroom teaching, the pivotal area, and five procedures for evaluating it are discussed: student evaluation, classroom visitation, teaching materials and procedures, special incident, and self-evaluation. Appendices include the North Carolina State computer experience with student evaluation and the research on the student appraisal of instruction form given in the book. An extensive selected and annotated bibliography is included.

MILLER, R. I., AND MUELLER, T. H. "A Study of Student Attitudes and Motivation in a Collegiate French Course Using Programmed Language Instruction." *International Review of Applied Linguistics,* 1970, *8,* 297–320.

One hundred and forty-nine students enrolled in French courses at the University of Kentucky responded on an extensive questionnaire as to their view on various aspects of the course, their attitudes toward the French people and their knowing the language, and their reactions toward aspects of programmed learning. A seventy-three-item questionnaire was administered anonymously at the end of the

1969 spring semester. A direct (and statistically significant) correlation was found between the number of hours spent outside of class on the course and the students' feelings of pleasantness, value, or ease. The higher the grade-point average the higher the percentage of those who recommended the course to other students—75 percent of those with a GPA of 2.6 to 3.4, and 92 percent of those above 3.4.

MOORE, R. "Structure of Faculty Attitudes Toward the University Teacher's Role: A Factor Analytic Study." *Educational and Psychological Measurement,* 1970, *30,* 293–299.

MORSH, J. E., AND OTHERS. "Student Achievement as a Measure of Instructor Effectiveness." *The Journal of Educational Psychology,* 1956, *47,* 79–88.

This study included 121 instructors in the aircraft mechanics course at Sheppard Air Force Base. Fourteen students were in each of the several tested units, which lasted eight days. These conclusions were made: student gains can be reliably measured; students know when they are well taught and therefore student ratings offer promise as a technique for instructor evaluation; students' rating of instructors' subject-matter knowledge was correlated significantly with instructors' proficiency test scores; little relationship was found between student gains and instructor intelligence or knowledge of subject matter; little relationship was found between supervisor or fellow instructor estimates of instructor effectiveness and student gains; and the high correlations found between fellow instructor and supervisor rankings, plus the fact that neither of these measures correlated highly with student gains, suggests that fellow instructors judge instructor effectiveness on the basis of factors other than student achievement.

MORTON, R. K. "Student Views of Teaching." *Improving College and University Teaching,* 1965, *13,* 140–142.

According to this article, student evaluation of teachers can be of use to the university administration, particularly to the academic dean, if it is used, along with other data, in evaluating a teacher's professional competence and teaching effectiveness in any given course and with a specific class. Proper allowance should be made for misinterpretation and possible frivolous or vindictive use by students.

MORTON, R. K. "Evaluating College Teaching." *Improving College and University Teaching,* 1961, *9,* 122–123.

Types of teaching evaluation are examined. Student evaluations, in spite of limitations and faults, can be quite helpful. Improvisations can also take place, such as the students' verbal discussion of the good and the bad aspects of teaching in the last class period or a written critique. Administrative visitation evaluation should be done on more than one occasion, and the evaluator should be supplied with course outline and be briefed in advance on course content, purposes, and procedures.

MUELLER, F. J. "Trends in Student Ratings of Faculty." *AAUP Bulletin,* 1951, *37,* 319–324.

The purpose of the study, based upon a survey of 804 colleges and universities in 1949, was to ascertain the extent to which student rating of teachers had grown. It was found that 26 percent of the colleges and universities were uninterested (34 percent for teachers colleges), 35 percent were interested short of trial (36 percent for teachers colleges), and 39 percent had experience with student ratings (30 percent for teachers colleges). The analysis revealed that publicly controlled institutions (exclusive of teachers colleges) showed the greatest interest. On the other hand, comparable independent and Protestant institutions lagged appreciably, and Catholic institutions were least interested; teachers colleges lagged behind in their interest and action; coeducational institutions manifested a considerably greater interest in student ratings than did their all-male and all-female counterparts; accredited institutions clearly exhibited a greater interest than did nonaccredited ones; interest in student ratings increased with the size of institution up to over 2,000, after which there was a slight decline; interest in student ratings was greatest in the central and western portions of the nation, and it diminished progressively as one proceeded from the South through the middle states to New England. To ascertain how institutions react to these ratings when they do try them, a further study was made of the 296 institutions which reported experience with the ratings. It was found that four out of five indicated plans to continue using the ratings. The same patterns of findings emerged from these data as were evident for the 804 samples with respect to type, size, and geographical location of institution. The author concludes "that never before has activity in this area even approached its present level intensity. What is more, this trend is still increasing."

MUSELLA, D., AND RUSCH, R. "Student Opinion on College Teaching." *Improving College and University Teaching*, 1968, *16*, 137–140.

Analysis of 394 student responses at the State University of New York at Albany indicated that the teaching behaviors which most promote thinking, in order of importance, were: (1) attitudes toward subject; (2) attitudes toward students; (3) effective use of questions; (4) speaking ability; (5) knowledge of subject; (6) organization of subject matter; and (7) extensive and effective use of discussion. Expert knowledge of subject was chosen frequently by students as an important characteristic associated with effective teaching in general. Systematic organization of subject matter and ability to explain clearly were among the top three behaviors in the physical and biological sciences, but ability to encourage thought and an enthusiastic attitude toward the subject were among the top three for the arts and social sciences.

NEELEY, M. "A Teacher's View of Teacher Evaluation." *Improving College and University Teaching*, 1968, *16*, 207–209.

Teachers have been rated and evaluated since the beginning of teaching and may expect to be evaluated in the future. But there is not, even in this day of standardized tests, a new and objective way of evaluating teachers. Authorities cannot agree as to what constitutes a good teacher. A review of the literature over the past twenty-five years indicates no objective usable criterion for identifying effective teachers.

NESS, F. W. *An Uncertain Glory*. San Francisco: Jossey-Bass, 1971.

NEWELL, D. *Evaluation of Teachers*. Lexington, Ky.: University of Kentucky, College of Dentistry Conference on Evaluation of Teaching and Teachers. Preconference readings, 1967.

The readings cover previous findings on the effectiveness of student evaluation of teaching. These studies investigated how ratings were obtained, if student qualified, and so forth. Conclusions indicate that: students are fairly good raters of their teachers; class size often affects ratings; only slight differences are evident in ratings for teachers of required and elective courses; students judge class procedures better than overall teaching ability; and in ranking instructors, degrees make a difference; and the quality of teaching in dental schools is good, but the need for improvement warrants serious consideration.

New Mexico State University. *Manual on the Explanation of Merit Rating System Rating Information Form*. Las Cruces, N.M., 1966.

Salary increases are granted by New Mexico State University on a merit basis. Each faculty member fills out a form annually. The evaluation is based on three kinds of contributions: teaching, research and/or creative scholarship, and professional service. The assigned duty load is considered in the final rating. The department head and others concerned make judgments to the best of their ability with the information at their command. Factors considered in evaluating teachers are: knowledge of subject matter, organization of material, attitude toward students, and attitude toward teaching. Points considered in connection with research and/ or creative scholarship are: preparation, planning and execution, results, and direction of graduate students. Factors considered in evaluation of professional service are: service with students, committee work—department, college and university, and off-campus professional work. Department heads study the information form, confer with the faculty member concerning strengths and weaknesses, confer with the appropriate dean, and assign a rating.

NOCHIMSON, R. L. "Student Rating of Faculty." AAUP *Bulletin.* A response to the McKeachie article in the December 1969 AAUP *Bulletin,* 1970, *56,* 6–7.

The author contends that the information derived from student ratings can be achieved by other means—even by mere guesswork. "I offer no statistical evidence, but, if someone still under thirty can make use of something as old-fashioned as a *feeling,* I should like to suggest that the atmosphere generated by having ratings of teachers submitted by their students to the administration seems likely to be an unhealthy one. The 'strong security measures' described by Professor McKeachie as necessary to preserve student anonymity suggest an atmosphere of suspicion and mistrust strangely out of keeping with the ideals of the university."

OHIO DEPARTMENT OF ELEMENTARY SCHOOL PRINCIPALS. *Evaluation of Administrators: Guidelines and Procedures.* Columbus, Ohio, 1971.

OZMON, H. "Publications and Teaching." *Improving College and University Teaching,* 1967, *15,* 106–107.

The author recommends that college and university faculties should be divided not only into departments but into two distinct sections within departments: one section for those who teach, and the other for those who do research and publishing, giving equal status to each, since one is no more important than the other. Thus a good teacher could become a full professor without publishing anything. The author also states that teacher self-evaluation is faulty: more weight should be placed on evaluation by students; faculty should be allowed to judge fellow staff members; and administrators need to be more energetic in evaluating teachers.

PACE, C. R. "Thoughts on Evaluation in Higher Education." *Essays on Education: No. 1,* Iowa City, Iowa: The American College Testing Program, 1972.

A concept of evaluation appropriate for the study of large and complex institutions is summarized. (1) It begins with the central question "What are the consequences?" rather than with the more limiting one "What are the objectives?" (2) Its style of inquiry is more aptly characterized by the word *exploration* than by the words *control* and *forms.* (3) It sees the role of the evaluator as that of a social scientist rather than that of a teacher, missionary, reformer, or staff officer to the practitioners. (4) Its purpose is to provide more complex bases for informed judgment. The author contends that "decision-making" is too narrow a focus for describing the purpose and role of evaluation, "explanation" is too abstract and impersonal, leaving "judgment" as the central orientation for evaluation studies.

PERRY, R. R. "Evaluation of Teaching Behavior Seeks to Measure Effectiveness." *College and University Business,* 1969, *47,* 18–22.

Thirteen thousand six hundred and forty-three responses from students, faculty, and alumni related to the University of Toledo were read by a jury and categorized into sixty effective teaching behaviors. These behaviors were then rated as to importance by 1793 students, faculty, and alumni. The twelve highest ratings were: being well prepared for class, establishing sincere interest in subject being taught, demonstrating comprehensive knowledge of the subject, using teaching methods which enable students to achieve objectives of the course, constructing tests which search for understanding on the part of students rather than rote memory ability, being fair and reasonable to students in evaluation procedures, communicating effectively at levels appropriate to the preparedness of students, organizing the course in logical fashion, motivating students to do their best, treating students with respect, and acknowledging all questions to the best of the teacher's ability.

PHILLIPS, B. N. "The 'Individual' and the 'Classroom Group' as Frames of Reference in Determining Teacher Effectiveness." *Journal of Educational Research,* 1964, *58,* 128–131.

The hypothesis that teaching effectiveness, determined by the uniform application of criteria, is different from teaching effectiveness determined by selective application of criteria is tested in this study. In other words, teacher effectiveness is measured by the extent to which what happens in the class agrees with what the student wants. Results indicated that students favored a highly structured class with "highly visible" tests over a highly motivating class with a strong emphasis on personal warmth. Additional evidence indicated that student characteristics play a crucial role in the perception of teacher effectiveness.

POGUE, F. G., JR. "Students' Ratings of the 'Ideal Teacher.'" *Improving College and University Teaching,* 1967, *15,* 133–136.

The University of Oregon evaluation form prepared by Quick and Wolf was used to determine the "ideal professor" at Philander Smith College. Forty-six percent (307 students) of the total college enrollment was polled. Characteristics listed as most important were: good knowledge of subject (41 percent); a good evaluator (14 percent); explains clearly (12 percent). Characteristics of the ideal teacher listed as least important were: is scholarly and participates actively in research (31 percent); likes college age youth (23 percent); has adequate and well-modulated voice (11 percent); and encourages independent thinking.

PRINCETON REPORT. "Report of the President's Committee for a Pilot Study in Student Evaluation at Princeton." In K. E. Eble, *The Recognition and Evaluation of Teaching*. Salt Lake City: Project to Improve College Teaching, 1259 East South Temple, 1970.

This report describes the process by which the Princeton Course Evaluation Booklet was developed, beginning in 1965 and going through several stages and steps. The instrument itself is given.

PUNKE, H. H. "Improvement in College Teaching." *Improving College and University Teaching*, 1965, *13,* 159–161.

To improve college teaching, as much objectivity as possible must be included in evaluation. Personal observations, interviews, opinionnaires, analysis of learned judgments, and similar evaluative devices are most helpful when they lean toward the overall objective and are used in relation to items listed on a point scale. The aims of a course, facilities, and conditions must be carefully considered in evaluative efforts.

QUERESHI, M. Y. "Teaching Effectiveness and Research Productivity." *Science*, 1968, *161,* 1160.

This annotation covers a critique made of an article by J. B. Bresler, which is annotated earlier in this bibliography. Quereshi contends that there are deficiencies in the methods of collecting data and in the analysis of the data. (1) It is well known that many students take two or more courses within their own field in any given semester; hence, the returns used as the basis of computing means and standard deviations for faculty receiving no support are not independent of each other. Reply by Bresler: the hypothesis of a departure from statistical independence is based on the assumption that there was systematic interrater bias. From the data available for this study, it could not be determined whether or not such a bias was operative. (2) No attempt was made to analyze the differences between means for various possible contrasts through use of a suitable statistical test, although several of the differences were substantial. Reply by Bresler: the alleged lack of independence would not affect the expected value of the mean scores but would affect the variance of the distribution of the means; a significance test would not add much. (3) On the basis of the information presented, it is not possible to conduct appropriate statistical tests, since it is not known whether the standard deviations that are reported represent variation within classes, variation across teachers' means, or some other estimate. Reply by Bresler: it is not clear whether Quereshi uses the word *classes* to represent courses or statistical groups. If the latter, the answer is contained in the data.

RAYDER, N. F. "College Student Ratings of Instructors." *The Journal of Experimental Education,* 1968, *37,* 76–81.

Results of a study of rating characteristics of 4285 college students at Colorado State College determined that: students remembered and accurately reported their grade point averages; ratings of instructors were not substantially related to student's sex, grade level, major area, GPA or grade(s) previously received from the instructor; and instructors who differ on certain characteristics were rated differently by their students.

REES, R. D. "Dimensions of Students' Points of View in Rating College Teachers." *Journal of Educational Psychology,* 1969, *60,* 476–482.

A factorial study was designed to yield "points of view" or "idealized individuals" with respect to the rating of college teachers. The eleven types of teachers representing seven academic areas were rated by sixty-nine students on twenty semantic differential scales. Seven factors representing different points of view in rating college teachers were identified through factor analysis. These were: socioeconomic, race, performance on social studies and other ACT tests, class level (freshman, and so forth), masculine sophistication level (as judged by ACT scores, travel, and view of teachers as unstructured), social disposition, and emotional stability. The study found that the concepts college students have of teachers are influenced in part by the personality traits and background experiences of the students themselves. Students from stable lower socioeconomic class homes are likely to be influenced more by their own predispositions than by teachers' behavior.

REMMERS, H. H., AND WEISBRODT, J. A. *Manual of Instructions for the Purdue Rating Scale for Instruction.* West Lafayette, Ind.: University Book Store, 1965.

This booklet, as well as the student response card and the rating scale, summarizes one-third of a century of use of the Purdue Rating Scale. The Purdue Rating Scale is perhaps the most widely-known scale; the bibliography in the manual begins with a 1927 entry. In addition, the manual outlines procedures for using available IBM equipment for computerized processing.

REMMERS, H. H. "Rating Methods in Research on Teaching." In N. L. Gage (Ed.), *Handbook of Research on Teaching.* Chicago: Rand McNally, 1963.

Objectivity, reliability, sensitivity, validity, and utility are five properties to look for in rating scales. Genera and species of rating scales and their properties are reviewed. Some issues and programs in research on teaching in which rating scales may be or have been applied are discussed and analyzed. Rating scales are categorized in five major groupings: numerical, graphic, standard, cumulated-points, and forced-choice.

REMMERS, H. H. "On Students' Perceptions of Teachers' Effectiveness." In W. J. McKeachie (Ed.), *The Appraisal of Teach-*

ing in Large Universities. Ann Arbor, Mich.: The University of Michigan Extension Service, 1959.

Teachers can be evaluated on either of two possible bases: (1) on the basis of changes they bring about in students, which is beset with many difficulties such as attributing the student achievement upon the efforts of a particular course and instructor; or (2) on the basis of those aspects of themselves that are assumed to be related to their effectiveness in bringing about desirable changes in students. The latter, of necessity, is the prevailing practice because characteristics of teachers (knowledge, skills, and attitudes) can be measured by a variety of tests and procedures. The author makes three general observations about evaluation of teaching: a teacher has no choice as to whether he wishes to be judged by students, and he only can exercise some control over the procedure itself and its usefulness in terms of his own teaching; student attitudes toward teachers strongly affects their learning; and students are the only ones who observe and are in a position to judge teaching effectiveness. Based upon some twenty studies conducted at Purdue in conjunction with the PRSI, eighteen conclusions are given:

(1) A considerable number of those who have used student ratings believe this procedure is useful for facilitating the educational process. (2) Knowledge of student opinions and attitudes leads to improvement of the teacher's personality and educational procedures. (3) There is some evidence that student opinion is positively related to achievement as measured by examination of students. (4) If twenty-five or more student ratings are averaged, they have as much reliability as do the better educational and mental tests available at present. (5) Grades of students are not in general closely related to the ratings of the teacher. (6) While the effect on student ratings of a generalized attitude ("halo effect") toward the teacher has not been isolated, it apparently does not exist to an extent sufficient to invalidate the ratings of separate aspects of teaching methods and of the course. Evidence indicates that students discriminate reliably

for different aspects of a teacher's personality and between different instructors and courses. (7) Little, if any, relationship exists between student rating and the judged difficulty of the course. (8) In a given institution there exist wide and important departmental differences in effectiveness of teaching as judged by student opinion. (9) The sex of the student rater bears little or no relationship to the ratings of teachers. (10) The cost in time and money of obtaining student opinions is lower than is the administration of a typical standardized educational test. (11) Popularity, apart from the class activities of the teacher, is probably not appreciably related to student ratings of that teacher. (12) No research has been published invalidating the use of student opinion as one criterion of teacher effectiveness. (13) A positive relationship (r .24) exists between students' achievements and ratings awarded after initial ability has been parcelled out. (14) Teachers with less than five years experience tend to be rated lower than are teachers with more than eight years experience. (15) The sex of the instructor has no effect on the ratings received. (16) The year in school of the rater has no effect on the ratings given except that ratings by graduate students tend to be higher than are those by undergraduates. (17) Students are more favorable to student ratings than are instructors, but more instructors have noticed improvement in their teaching as a result of student ratings than the students have. (18) Mature alumni of ten years' standing agree substantially with on-campus students in their evaluation of teachers.

Only the instructor concerned should have the results of evaluation, and only at the instructor's option should an administrator have them.

REMMERS, H. H. "Reliability and Halo Effect of High School and College Students' Judgments of Their Teachers." *Journal of Applied Psychology*, 1934, *18*, 619–630.

The sampling included ratings of fifty-seven high school practice teachers and seventy-six college instructors, with these conclusions: reliable judgments of classroom traits of instructors can be obtained from both high school and college students; the traits investigated—the three most important of the ten on the Purdue Scale: interest in subject, presentation of subject matter, and stimulating intellectual curiosity—have very little psychological interdependence; it is probable that high school students will invest the practice teacher with less halo than college students will their instructors.

REMMERS, H. H. "To What Extent Do Grades Influence Student Ratings of Instructors?" *Journal of Educational Research,* 1930, *21,* 314–317.

Correlation of grades against student ratings for 409 students under eleven different instructors in seventeen different classes varying widely in subject matter gives correlations for individual traits of individual teachers varying from —.86 to +.89. The correlations when averaged by traits vary from —.06 to +.14, with the average of all correlations being +.07. The conclusion seems inescapable, therefore, that for the average instructor and the average student there is practically no relationship between the student's grades and his judgment of the teacher as recorded on the Purdue Rating Scale. (This report is an elaboration upon an earlier one by the same author: "The Relationship Between Students' Marks and Student Attitude Toward Instructors." *School and Society,* 1928, *28,* 759–760.)

REMMERS, H. H., AND BRANDENBURG, G. C. "Experimental Data on the Purdue Rating Scale for Instruction." *Educational Administration and Supervision,* 1927, *13,* 519–527.

"The Purdue Rating Scale . . . purports to measure the students' judgments of the instructor on the ten categories given on the scale. To the extent that students agree among themselves on the amount of the trait which the instructor possesses, and, more important, the extent to which each student is self-consistent in his judgments, to that extent we are in position to say that the scale is valid. For this scale reliability is synonymous with validity." Based upon a research study using two forms with items differently arranged and used by three different instructors, the statistical analysis indicated that student judgments as measured by the PRSI "have a considerable degree of reliability." The results also indicated that students discriminated successfully among various traits for the same instructor and among different instructors for the same trait.

RENNER, R. R. "A Successful Rating Scale." *Improving College and University Teaching,* 1967, *15,* 12–14.

Students, as the ultimate consumers of the teacher's efforts, know best whether he has been effective or not. They are not trained judges of the suitability of their mentor's methods, but they do judge whether or not the course had value for them. Although their reactions are not the only index of teacher competence, they appear to be most sharply focused on teaching itself, both its content and process. A college administrator usually evaluates teaching largely on the basis of casual reports from students and faculty members. With these factors in mind, a faculty-approved rating scale was devised, and is included.

REPORT OF A COMMITTEE OF THE UNIVERSITY OF MICHIGAN CHAPTER OF THE AAUP. *The Evaluation of Faculty Services.* Ann Arbor, Mich.: University of Michigan Administrative Services, Vol. 1, No. 3, 1939.

The Committee recommended that these faculty activities be evaluated as follows: (1) teaching ability to be judged by visitation to classes, by colleagues whose individual judgments are to be combined to give a composite opinion, and by students through the proposed questionnaire; (2) research to be judged by the department in such a way as it deems best and as often as need arises or when requested by an administrative officer; (3) standing in profession to be appraised by colleagues, by outside men, and by department head on basis of participation in learned societies; (4) personal qualities to be appraised by colleagues, a composite opinion to be developed by combining individual opinions; (5) value in departmental and university administration to be stated by department head; and (6) value of public and community services to be stated by department head or committee.

Report of the Committee on Evaluation. Fort Worth: Texas Christian University, 1971.

RODIN, M., AND RODIN, B. "Student Evaluations of Teachers." *Science* Magazine, 1972, *177*, 1164–1166.

The study used 293 students in a large undergraduate calculus course which was taught by a professor who lectured three times a week and by teaching assistants on two days. There were twelve sections, two of which were taught by the same instructor. Three measures were obtained for each section: initial ability in calculus, amount learned by the students, and student evaluation of the instructor. "The major defense for defining good teaching in terms of good scores on the student evaluation forms is based on an analogy between the student and the consumer—the student, as the primary consumer of the teaching product, is in the best position to evaluate its worth. However, the present data indicate that students are less than perfect judges of teaching effectiveness if the latter is measured by how much they have learned. If how much students learn is considered to be a major component of good teaching, it must be concluded that good teaching is not validly measured by student evaluations in their current form." (For a critique, see Centra, Oct. 17, 1972, unpublished letter.)

ROVIN, S. (Ed.). *Evaluation of Teaching and Teachers.* Lexington, Ky.: University of Kentucky, College of Dentistry. Proceedings of the Faculty Conference, 1967.

Student evaluation, peer evaluation, administrative evaluation, alumni evaluation, and self-evaluation are discussed. Reports in these areas indicate the following: (1) student evaluation of subject matter competency should be viewed with caution; pedagogical skills are evaluated by students more easily, and professional attitudes and habits are the easiest areas for students to observe (relevance is questioned); (2) voluntary selection of peers was mentioned, secrecy was deplored, objectives of the technique were questioned, and the need of provisions to inform the administration of inadequate department chairmen was discussed; (3) a system of assistance and correction is needed for administration evaluation instead of reward or punishment, the department chairman plays a critical role which must be defined, and the dean should serve as appellate authority; (4) the utilization of conferences and questionnaires for alumni evaluation was explored; (5) self-evaluation should be a conscious process and utilized continuously—it should not be used, by itself, to justify monetary or academic rank advancements.

ROWLAND, R. "Can Teaching Be Measured Objectively?" *Improving College and University Teaching,* 1970, *18,* 153–157.

The author states that each approach to evaluation has its place as well as its limitations and shortcomings. None will work effectively in an unfriendly atmosphere. A good atmosphere will prevail only when assessment of instruction is regarded throughout the academic community as a means of accomplishing overall improvement rather than as a threat to individuals. Because of the nature of college teaching, its measurement can never be entirely accurate and objective, but with effort and cooperation from all involved, measurement can be made less haphazard and subjective than it is now.

ROYCE, J. E. "Popularity and the Teacher." *Education,* 1956, *77,* 233–237.

The author contends that a paradox of teaching is that the teacher must be popular; yet to aim at popularity is perhaps the greatest mistake a teacher can make. In order to be effective in one's work with students, one must be acceptable; yet to aim at acceptability frequently spoils any possibility for effectiveness. A small research study was conducted to compare student ratings with general popularity. The findings indicate that students are very demanding of their teachers; and the amount of work and the standards of performance which the teacher requires are better indices of his standing in the pupil's eyes than is his superficial personality attractiveness.

RUSSELL, H. E., AND BENDIG, A. W. "An Investigation of the Relation of Student Ratings of Psychology Instructors to their Course Achievement When Academic Aptitude Is Controlled." *Educational and Psychological Measurement,* 1953, *13,* 626–635.

A regression equation was devised to predict letter grades of students in an introductory psychology course from ACE scores. Students were divided into three groups on the basis of the discrepancy between their predicted and obtained grades: A "plus" group consisting of students whose obtained grade was more than one-half standard error of estimate above their predicted grade; an "equal" group whose obtained grade was within one-half a standard error of their predicted grade; and a "minus" group whose actual achievement fell more than one-half a standard error below their expected grade. Analysis of the students' ratings of their instructors on the Miami Instructor Rating Sheet indicated that no overall difference existed between the "plus" and the "minus" groups in their ratings of the instructors, but that relative achievement (residual achievement of students when their aptitude is statistically controlled) affected single scales on the Miami Scale. Significantly more favorable ratings were given by the "plus" groups on rating scales measuring attitude toward the course, but relative achievement had little effect on student attitudes toward the instructors. Little relation was found between measures of instructor effectiveness derived from pooled students' ratings and from pooled measures of their relative achievement.

RYANS, D. G. "Teacher Behavior Can Be Evaluated." In *The Evaluation of Teaching*. Washington, D.C.: Pi Lambda Theta, 1967. Betty J. Humphry, colloquy moderator.

The behavioral components of teaching are: motivating and reinforcing, organizing and managing, presenting and demonstrating, evaluating, and counseling and advising. The author makes the following seven assumptions with respect to the premise that teaching can be evaluated: teacher behavior is characterized by lawfulness and order; empirical study and inductive inference (scientific induction) provide a valid approach to the understanding of teacher behavior; teacher behavior is observable; individual differences exist in observable teacher behavior; teacher behavior is social in nature; the ultimate goal or end product of teacher behavior is a set of specified pupil behaviors; and teacher behavior is relative. Research by Ryans and his associates indicates three prominent patterns of observable classroom behavior: pattern X (friendly, understanding, sympathetic teacher behavior); pattern Y (responsible, businesslike, systematic teacher behavior); and pattern Z (stimulating, imaginative teacher behavior).

RYDER, S. "Evaluating the Teacher." *Improving College and University Teaching*, 1970, *18*, 272–274.

One teacher's experience with a narrative-type student appraisal of an English I course is summarized. From that, he learned: don't expect too many ideas from students; at the risk of boring yourself, be a little redundant; not every misinterpretation or dropout is your fault; ask students for an evaluation early in the term when you can remedy some misunderstandings before it is too late.

SAMALONIS, B. "Ratings By Students." *Improving College and University Teaching,* 1967, *15,* 11.

The author believes that student ratings should be available as a basis for faculty advancement.

SAMPLE, S. B. "Inherent Conflict Between Research and Education. *Educational Record,* 1972, *53,* 17–22.

Most major universities, according to the author, refuse to face the conflict between research and education, either claiming that the two are equally important or publicly supporting education while privately favoring research. "The most unfortunate aspect of the conflict between research and education is that, left unresolved, it pits the professor against the student in a contest difficult for either to win. The faculty member assumes that research is the principal goal and therefore views most of his student contacts as potential threats to his professional aspirations. The student, on the other hand, thinks development of his mind and intellect should be the central concern of the university and feels cheated upon finding that most professors do not share this concern."

SCHMITT, H. A. "Teaching and Research: Companions or Adversaries?" *Journal of Higher Education,* 1965, *36,* 419–427.

Using insight in the account of his own problems and dilemmas as a young Ph.D., the author contends that good teaching is a matter of talent plus enthusiasm and no amount of public exhortation is going to produce either. Any individual who accepts his discipline as he finds it cannot be an adequate teacher. The young Ph.D. who looks forward to being a good teacher must plan a program of continuous research to keep in intellectual trim. The two are inseparable. A good teacher inspires and exploits curiosity, and he cannot do this if he lacks this precious quality himself.

SCHWARTZ, R. "Student Power—In Response to the Questions."

ment of Instruction in Higher Education, Report to the American Association of Colleges for Teacher Education, Washington, D.C.: 1962b.

The 487 representatives of AACTE were given a list of seventeen teacher self-evaluation tools. Requests for the questionnaire were so numerous that eventually 5303 of them were available for analysis. The highest ranked approach on the list was the "comparative check on your efficiency using one teaching approach versus your efficiency using another approach." However, the item with the highest success ratio was "voluntary and continuing colleague discussions or seminars by instructors of a particular course." Conclusions drawn as a result of the study were: (1) the tools judged most successful for self-evaluation in terms of information gathering are teacher oriented rather than student oriented; (2) lack of knowledge about the process of self-evaluation is a restraining factor; (3) the use of self-evaluative tools is dependent upon the subject matter field involved; and (4) an extremely small fraction of college instructors react almost violently to any self-evaluation proposal.

SLOBIN, D. Y., AND NICHOLS, D. G. "Student Rating of Teaching." *Improving College and University Teaching,* 1969, *17,* 244–248.

Although faculty has commonly opposed student rating of teaching, after a few years of experience, most of them have come to accept and even praise it. The article refutes these common objections to student rating: student ratings are influenced by variables irrelevant to teaching; student ratings reflect only the instructor's personality; students cannot evaluate the goals of teaching; a man should be judged by his peers; and overemphasis on teaching has bad consequences.

SMART, R. C. *The Evaluation of Teaching Performance from the Point of View of the Teaching Profession.* Chicago: American Psychological Association Meeting, 1965.

How did the AAUP feel about teaching evaluation in 1965?

Various positions, principles, and committee reports are given. In reviewing the work of the AAUP, it was found that no committee had been formulated specifically to study evaluation procedures. Previous association statements relate that freedom of teaching has to do primarily with the selection of topics to be covered in a given course. Evaluation of instruction may be done by the college administration but is better done by colleagues, who are in a better position to judge the dignity, courtesy and temperateness of language, the patience, considerateness, and pedagogical wisdom employed.

SMITH, R., AND FIEDLER, F. E. "The Measurement of Scholarly Work: A Critical Review of the Literature." *Educational Record*, 1971, *52*, 225–232.

Several criteria are required for a good evaluation of publications and research. The place and frequency of citation of the work seems to be least contaminated by such factors as the prestige of the scholar's university or the sheer number of papers published. Other factors studied, and found to be useful, were productivity, recognition, and journal quality.

SNOW, R. H. "The Precarious State of Teaching." *Journal of Higher Education*, 1963, *34*, 318–323.

The author contends that faculty members are increasingly inclined to devote a major share of their efforts to many enterprises outside the classroom, allowing their energies to be diverted from teaching. Recognizing publication as the route to academic advancement, they struggle to produce the book and articles which they hope will justify their claims to promotion and prestige. They negotiate research contracts, serve as paid consultants, and conduct private business ventures on the side. Few rewards or distinctions seem to accrue to those who excel as teachers. Under such circumstances, there is a very real and ever-present hazard that the caliber of teaching within colleges will not be maintained at the highest levels of excellence and may even deteriorate.

SOLOMON, D. "Teacher Behavior Dimensions, Course Characteristics, and Student Evaluations of Teachers." *American Educational Research Journal,* 1966, *3,* 35–47.

Students of 229 teachers of evening college courses filled out questionnaires near the end of a semester describing the behavior of the teachers and evaluating their teaching. The within-class item means from these questionnaires were factor-analyzed, producing ten factors: (1) lecturing versus encouragement of broad, expressive student participation; (2) energy and facility of communication versus lethargy and vagueness; (3) criticism, disapproval, and hostility versus tolerance; (4) control and factual emphasis versus permissiveness; (5) warmth and approval versus coldness; (6) obscurity and difficulty of presentation versus clarity; (7) dryness versus flamboyance; (8) precision and organization versus informality; (9) nervousness versus relaxation; and (10) impersonality versus personal expression. Relationships were investigated between the teachers' factor scores and student evaluations, with significant relationships with factors (1) and (2); class size, with no significant relationships; "basic" versus "applied" courses, with significant relationships with factors (1), (3), and (9); and course area (social science, humanities, mathematics and natural science, and applied science), with significant relationships with factors (1), (4), (5), (6), (9) and (10).

SOLOMON, D., AND OTHERS. "Teacher Behavior and Student Learning." *Journal of Educational Psychology,* 1964, *55,* 23–30.

Classroom behavior of twenty-four teachers of evening college courses in introductory American government was measured with tape recordings and observers' ratings of two class sessions, student descriptive questionnaires, and teacher questionnaires. Factor analysis of these measures produced eight factors. These were then related to students' learning (measured by pre- and post-tests) and to student evaluations. Learning of facts was significantly related to teacher "clarity, expressiveness," and to "lecturing"—both efficient for factual information transmission. Gains in comprehension related significantly to teacher "energy, flamboyance," and a moderate position on a permissiveness versus control continuum—all having to do with activating students' interest and personal involvement. Student evaluations related significantly to "clarity, expressiveness" and to "warmth."

SOREY, K. E. "A Study of the Distinguishing Personality Characteristics of College Faculty Who Are Superior in Regard to the Teaching Function." *Dissertation Abstracts,* 1968, *28* (12-A), 4916.

Fifty college teachers were rated by their students on the Purdue Rating Scale and were divided into two groups, the upper 26 percent and the lower 26 percent, and three hypotheses were tested: (1) superior teachers, as rated by their students, will score in the socially valued direction on a greater number of the Guilford-Zimmerman traits than will inferior teachers; (2) superior teachers will show a more positive self-concept, that is, rate themselves more positively on the Self-Rating Scale than will the inferior teachers; (3) superior teachers will show more accuracy in their self-ratings, as measured by the discrepancy between self-rating and Guilford-Zimmerman scores, than will inferior teachers. Hypotheses (1) and (3) were not confirmed, and only provisional support was obtained for the second hypothesis. The data revealed that superior teachers possess some characteristics which are commonly believed to be associated with inferior teachers. Superior teachers conceive of themselves, in terms of personality characteristics, quite similarly to the inferior teachers, possibly reflecting a common role conception. Superior teachers do not estimate their personality characteristics as accurately as do inferior teachers, which may be partly a result of the method of assessing accuracy—essentially a discrepancy between teacher conception and student conception of the college teacher role in terms of personality characteristics. It shows that the characteristics commonly valued by the teachers themselves are associated, by the students, with inferior teachers.

SORTAIN, A. Q., AND WARING, E. G. "Interest in and Value of College Courses." *Journal of Applied Psychology*, 1944, *28*, 520–526.

Two attitude scales, one for interest in and another for value of college subjects, were built by the method of equal-appearing intervals. These scales were then administered to 504 students of English, government, psychology, and social science at Southern Methodist University, with these conclusions: The reliability of the scales was moderate but satisfactory. Because the scales showed significant differences between both subjects and instructors and because most of the differences seem reasonable to one who knows the prevailing student opinion, scales probably have some validity. There were, in the opinion of the students, differences in the interest value and in the general value of college courses, although it is not presumed that the order found in this study was necessarily correct. Differences between instructors seemed to be even greater than were differences between departmental subjects. The relationship between interest in college courses and marks received in them was negligible. And interest in courses and value of courses were fairly closely related (.702).

SPAIGHTS, E. "Students Appraise Teachers' Methods and Attitudes." *Improving College and University Teaching*, 1967, *15*, 15–17.

A study of student-teacher appraisal looked for answers to two questions: (1) Do high-achieving students have more favorable perceptions of instructors' teaching methods than do low-achieving students? (2) Do high-achieving students view the personal attitudes of college instructors more favorably than do low-achieving students? Two samples (293 students) were examined. Results indicated that students with both high and low grade-point averages thought there was too much emphasis on the lecture method. Both groups agreed that there was a general lack of independent study. The low-achieving group felt that too much emphasis was being placed on mastery of the textbook, while the above-average students favored greater use of audio-visual aids than did those below average. Above-average students wanted more essay examinations. The majority of the low-achieving students perceived the typical college instructor as being impersonal, dictatorial, sarcastic, and lacking enthusiasm in his work, while few high-achieving students saw instructors as having many undesirable personality traits.

SPENCER, R. E., AND ALEAMONI, L. M. "A Student Course Evaluation Questionnaire." *Journal of Educational Measurement,* 1970, *7,* 209–210.

This article describes an instrument which elicits student opinions about a standardized set of statements relative to certain aspects of an instructional program, and the norms which enable an instructor to compare his results with the results of other instructors. This version of the Illinois Course Evaluation Questionnaire (CEQ) consisted of fifty short statements to which the student responded by indicating his agreement or disagreement on a four-point scale. Normative data were established on more than one hundred thousand students, two thousand course sections, and four hundred different courses. Administrations of the CEQ to a number of institutions indicate that the normative data are relatively stable from institution to institution.

STECKLEIN, J. E. "Colleges and Universities—Programs (Evaluation)." In C. W. Harris (Ed.), *Encyclopedia of Educational Research.* New York: Macmillan, 1960.

Evaluation is defined as a deliberate effort to match the purposes of an activity against various evidences which suggest how far these purposes have been attained and then to draw conclusions regarding the adequacy of the means used and of the ends themselves. The four approaches to the evaluational effectiveness that provide the most direct appraisal are: consideration of study guides, examinations, and other materials prepared for teaching purposes; ratings by administrators or colleagues; student ratings; and evidences of actual student achievement. Most student rating forms to date have been used on a voluntary basis and for the improvement of instruction rather than for promotional or other administrative reasons. Very few appraisals based on the opinions of colleagues have been reported in the literature. The assessment of teaching competence is a much more complex procedure than the early investigators believed.

STEWART, C. T., AND MALPASS, L. F. "Estimates of Achievement and Ratings of Instructors." *Journal of Educational Research*, 1966, *59*, 347–350.

Here is a synopsis of the results of a study in which a course and instructor information form was administered by sixty-seven instructors teaching fifty-four courses to 1975 students. Analysis of the questionnaires showed that of the students sampled, those expecting higher grades graded their instructors significantly higher than did those expecting low grades. Freshmen viewed grading policies more favorably than did upperclass students. Further analysis indicated that instructors should consider reducing the complexity of their classroom presentation for freshmen and increasing the sophistication of their presentation for upper classmen.

STUIT, D. B. "Needed Research on the Evaluation of Instructional Effectiveness." In W. J. McKeachie (Ed.), *The Appraisal of Teaching in Large Universities*. Ann Arbor, Mich.: The University of Michigan Extension Service, 1959.

Several areas are outlined that require research and study: faculty attitudes toward evaluation; measurement of changes in student behavior through achievement tests, measures of critical thinking and problem solving, better test norms, and measures of changes in attitudes and appreciations; ways and means of developing better methods of observation and rating; relationships between scholarly productivity and quality of teaching; and better definition of good teaching.

STUIT, D. B., AND EBEL, R. L. "Instructor Rating at a Large State University." *College and University*, 1952, *27*, 247–254.

The article reports the results of three studies at the University of Iowa from 1948 to 1950. In the first study, 1,230 students answered about their competency to rate an instructor in these categories: knowledge of his subject, 57 percent answered "yes;" clarity in explaining points, 95 percent; interest in class progress, 81 percent; friendliness and co-operativeness, 94 percent; enthusiasm for his subject, 88 percent; and fairness in examinations, 68 percent. With respect to who should see the results of the student ratings, students answered: the dean for use in evaluating instructors' work, 2 percent; the instructor for his use in improving his instruction, 36 percent, and both, 62 percent. And when asked if positive benefits were likely from the ratings, 92 percent of the students replied in the affirmative. A second study received responses from 150 faculty members. They favored (87 percent) receiving a systematic evaluation by students; and 48 percent believed that the dean, the department head, and the instructor should have rating available to them, as compared with 0 percent for the dean only, 4 percent for the department head only, and 36 percent for the instructor only. The third study analyzed the results of 7,559 rating sheets for instructors in 267 classes. Students credit full professors with more knowledge of their subject, and with more interest in it, but with less tolerance and helpfulness than instructors of other ranks.

TAYLOR, P. S. "Student Rating of Faculty." AAUP *Bulletin*, 1970, *56*, 7–8. A response to the McKeachie article in the December 1969 AAUP *Bulletin*.

"Only students who are really in touch with their experiences are capable of delivering an effective, and therefore *valuable,* evaluation of any instructor. . . . Grades in any form should be opposed by all thinking faculty, for themselves as well as for students. I would suggest, as Socrates does, that public opinion should not be listened to because one cannot hold it responsible for its views." At Wayne State, students who are perceptive and "experimentally in touch" sit in on classes and then write an evaluation. One week is sufficient. Each of these selected students evaluates about forty courses a quarter, and each evaluation appears in a course evaluation book. Faculty are also invited to supply information which may aid students in choosing courses or instructors. And thirdly, a short form dealing with general areas of the class is given to students in the classroom.

TREFFINGER, D. J., AND FELDHUSEN, J. F. "Predicting Students' Ratings of Instruction." *Proceedings of the 78th Annual Convention of the American Psychological Association,* 1970, *5,* 621–622.

This study examined the correlates of students' ratings but differs from some previous studies in that it used multivariate rather than univariate techniques. In addition, several different kinds of student variables were used, including cognitive and personality characteristics, specific and general attitude measures, and course performance indexes. One hundred ninety-two Purdue University undergraduates enrolled in an introductory educational psychology course participated in this study. Emerging from these data is the relative importance of the generalized precourse ratings (and particularly, of taking the PRSI at the very beginning of the course) as predictors of specific course and instructor ratings.

TUCKMAN, B. W., AND OLIVER, W. F. "Effectiveness of Feedback to Teachers as a Function of Source." *Journal of Educational Psychology,* 1968, *59,* 297–301.

The sample consisted of 286 teachers of vocational subjects at the high school or technical institute level, and the teachers were categorized by years of teaching experience and subjected to one of four conditions: feedback from students only; from supervisors, that is, vice-principals only; from both students and supervisors; and from neither (no feedback). It was found that student feedback led to a positive change among teachers, as measured by change in students' ratings across a twelve-week interval.

Feedback from supervisors alone produced a significantly negative shift in a direction opposite from that of student feedback. Student feedback improved teacher behavior as compared to no feedback. Supervisor feedback produced no additional effect when combined with student feedback.

TYLER, R. W. "The Evaluation of Teaching." In R. M. Cooper (Ed.), *The Two Ends of the Log*. Minneapolis: University of Minnesota Press, 1958.

Four procedures for evaluating teaching are discussed: a tape recorder in the classroom and subsequent private playback which can help check on some classroom conditions that may escape memory; classroom visitation; student evaluation; and an analysis of teaching materials and resources. On student evaluation, the author writes that students can report on their interest in the course, on their understanding of what is expected of them, on their satisfaction with achievement in the field, on the amount and extent of their study, and so forth. There are other important aspects of effective teaching which the students are not in a good position to judge such as the soundness of the objectives, the validity of the reference material provided, and the relevance of the approach.

UNIVERSITY OF OREGON. "Projected System for Publishing Ratings of Teachers." Unpublished memorandum. Eugene, Ore. No date given.

The university made the following resolution after studying the problem of whether a system could be devised for publishing and distributing student ratings of a teacher against his will: "Systematic survey of student reaction to courses and instruction at the university would be welcomed and faculty assistance would be provided if requested. Furthermore, any evaluation may be published against the will of any faculty member, provided the faculty member states his position before publication time."

UNIVERSITY OF NEVADA, LAS VEGAS. *Student Evaluation of Faculty.* Las Vegas: The University, 1972.

There were two main objectives in this university-wide faculty evaluation: to provide feedback to instructional personnel concerning students' opinions about the quality of university courses as well as the adequacy of instruction on the campus, and to enable students to learn in advance something about the courses they would be taking as well as about the professors teaching these courses. The committee charged with the project took precautions to protect the anonymity of students and professors. The professors' names and courses were coded and a procedure was employed so that the student summarizers and committee members did not know which instructors or which courses were being considered during the summarization procedure. The student writers had four inputs to consider in their summaries: the professor's comments about the course, the demographic data on the computer printouts, the statistical data on the printouts, and the handwritten student comments on the questionnaires. Faculty advisors supervised the summarization procedure. The seventy-one-page booklet contains the name of the professor who taught the course, the title of the course, course enrollment, narrative comment, and the professor's ratings on twenty-five questions.

UNIVERSITY OF WASHINGTON REPORT. "University of Washington Report of the ad hoc Committee on Student Evaluation of Teaching." In K. E. Eble, *The Recognition and Evaluation of Teaching.* Salt Lake City: Project to Improve College Teaching, 1259 East South Temple, 1970.

The Report from the University of Washington, 1968, presents a plan for implementation of recommendation of the Council on Academic Standards for expanded use of student evaluation of teaching. Several positive suggestions for improving the teaching program are presented and particular attention is given to the guidance and supervision of teaching assistants.

VAN WAES, R. "Student Freedoms and Educational Reform." *Stress and Campus Response: Current Issues in Higher Education.* San Francisco: Jossey-Bass, 1968.

Student complaints must be heard to determine the sources of their frustration and dissatisfaction. Students object to curriculum; they desire relevance, commitment, and leverage. They object to teaching methods. They reject "canned knowledge," "packaged formulae," "learning by fiat," and the lack of "genuine" dialogue. If students can criticize and actually share in the governance of their colleges, there will be an opportunity to confront institutional problems in a context that is both less dramatic and less explosive, and probably more fruitful.

VOEKS, V. W. "Publications and Teaching Effectiveness." *The Journal of Higher Education* 1962, *33,* 212–218.

A study was made of over two thousand students and two groups of 305 and 193 faculty members at the University of Washington to learn more about publications and research. Statistical comparisons were undertaken for relationships between extensiveness of publishing and effectiveness of teaching. No relationship was found for any academic rank or for any academic area. The two do not go hand in hand, but neither do they ordinarily conflict; they simply are unrelated in any apparent way.

VOEKS, V. W., AND FRENCH, G. M. "Are Student-Ratings of Teachers Affected by Grades?" *Journal of Higher Education,* 1960, *31,* 330–334.

Student ratings for 299 faculty members at the University of Washington were gathered in 1952 to ascertain the relationship between student grades received and student ratings given. The differences were so insignificant that the researchers concluded that higher ratings cannot be bought by giving high grades, nor are they lost by giving low grades. Both when judging an instructor's overall value as a teacher and when rating his skills in specific respects, such as clarity of presentation and development of interest, the students rarely were influenced by the grades which they had received from the teacher.

WALKER, B. D. "An Investigation of Selected Variables Relative to the Manner in Which a Population of Junior College Students Evaluate their Teachers." *Dissertation Abstracts,* 1969, *29* (9-B), 3474.

The sample included 1,447 student rating forms of thirty teachers at Lee Junior College in 1967, with these conclusions: students tend to rate teachers higher when the courses are what students expect; there is no relationship between the difficulty of the course as perceived by students and the manner in which they evaluate teachers; students tend to give higher ratings to teachers who teach courses which students believe are fulfilling their needs; the sex of the student or of the teacher is not a factor in student ratings; older students tend to rate teachers higher than do younger students; more experienced teachers tend to get higher ratings than do less experienced ones; female students rate female teachers significantly higher than male teachers; and teachers of mathematics and science receive higher ratings than do teachers of other subjects.

WALSH, W. B. "Validity of Self-Report." *Journal of Counseling Psychology,* 1967, *14,* 18–23.

A study of 270 male undergraduate students at the University of Iowa sought to determine the comparative accuracies of three forms of self-reporting: the questionnaire, the interview, and the personal data form. No differences between scores were found for the three methods across both control and experimental populations. The results indicate that no one method elicits more accurate self-reporting than does another. The study also indicates that an experimental financial incentive to distort has little effect on the accuracy of the self-reports for the items used in this study.

WARRINGTON, W. G. "The MSU Student Instructional Rating System (SIRS)." Paper given at an American Educational Research Association Symposium, Chicago, Apr. 4, 1972.

The SIRS was developed over a two-year period, beginning in 1967, and continues to undergo modification and change. The instrument has been administered to over four hundred thousand students on the Michigan State University (MSU) campus. (Steps in the two years of development of SIRS are available through the Office of Evaluation Services, 202 South Kedzie Hall, MSU, East Lansing, Mich. 48823.) After university-wide examination of SIRS, the University Academic Council at MSU passed a resolution with two features of particular interest: The resolution made the use of SIRS mandatory across the board, and the resolution officially recognized that student reactions to instructors are no longer the sole property of the particular faculty member but belong, in part, to that segment of the university involved in making decisions with respect to academic effectiveness of the individual faculty member. Any system of evaluation must be internally reinforcing if it is to be self-improving. The components of SIRS will be internally reinforcing to the extent that the form is acceptable as useful and the report is relevant and understandable. But to make the system complete, offices and facilities must be established which will provide positive assistance to those who have a need for assistance in instructional improvement. MSU has established learning services that are addressed to instructional improvement for individual instructors.

WEAVER, C. H. "Instructor Rating by College Students." *Journal of Educational Psychology,* 1960, *51,* 21–25.

Two questions were investigated: do students, when rating an instructor, tend to give him about the same kind of grade that they expect to receive in the course, and is student criticism of the instructor directed toward both his personality and teaching skill? The research found in a sample of 699 students (thirty-nine classes in four disciplines) that student ratings of instructors were biased in the direction of the grades which they received in the course; most student bias was directed toward teaching skills and abilities of the instructor; student ratings of the instructors' teaching skill did not seem to be a product of a popularity halo; and students who expected to receive C's seemed to be generally less discriminating in their appraisal than were those who expected to receive A's or B's.

WEBB, W. B., AND NOLAN, C. Y. "Student, Supervisor, and Self-Ratings of Instructional Proficiency." *The Journal of Educational Psychology,* 1955, *46,* 42–46.

Fifty-one instructors in the Naval Air Technical Training School at Jacksonville, Florida, were rated by both students and supervisors on a teaching proficiency rating scale. In addition, the instructors rated themselves on the same scale. It was found that the student ratings and the instructor self-ratings were highly correlated. However, the supervisor's ratings were uncorrelated with any of the additional measures obtained: intelligence, level of schooling, teaching experience, or desire to teach. There was a tendency for the more intelligent instructors, and those with more schooling, to be more self-critical. Those who expressed a greater desire to teach were rated as superior teachers by their students. The discrepany between student ratings and the instructor's ratings did not seem to be related to the judged proficiency of the teacher.

WERDELL, P. *Course and Teacher Evaluation.* Washington, D.C.: United States National Student Association, 1966.

Various methods for dealing with course and teacher evaluation are described. Included in material are evaluation forms, questionnaires, discussions, and positions.

WILLIAMS, R. L. *The Administration of Academic Affairs in Higher Education.* Ann Arbor, Mich.: The University of Michigan Press, 1965.

Sustained evaluation should focus on the three faculty functions of teaching, research, and public service. Contributions in these areas cannot be readily assessed by members of the administrative staff; they are more properly evaluated by faculty. Even then, however, there is no guarantee that judgments will be infallible or that everyone will be satisfied with the outcome. Faculty ratings do occur; opinions are expressed; evaluations are made. Teaching is the most difficult function to evaluate. One would expect that outstanding performance in teaching or research or public service, with acceptable performance in the other two areas, would be sufficient to indicate that recommendation for promotion is appropriate.

WILSON, R. C., AND DIENST, E. R. *Users Manual. Teacher Description Questionnaires:* Berkeley, Calif.: Center for Research and Development in Higher Education, 1971.

This manual provides basic information necessary for administering and scoring its questionnaires and suggests possible modifications for adapting the general formats to meet local circumstances. The questionnaires were developed as part of a study of teaching and teacher evaluation conducted by the Center. (See HILDEBRAND AND OTHERS for a more complete review of this study.) Each form provides a description of teaching and an evaluation of teaching effectiveness. Scales and items focus on a description of teaching and provide the individual instructor with a profile of his behavior as perceived by students or colleagues, while the evaluation questions provide information on the overall perceived effectiveness of his teaching practices. There are four teacher description questionnaires available: two are based on student evaluations and two on colleague evaluations; and a medium and short form is available for each. The manual contains sections on adapting the questionnaire to local circumstances, uses of the questionnaire, administering and scoring, and interpreting the teacher description profiles.

WILSON, R. C., AND OTHERS. "Characteristics of Effective College Teachers as Perceived by Their Colleagues." Unpublished manuscript. Berkeley, Calif.: Center for Research and Development in Higher Education, 1969.

This study explored some characteristics which faculty members ascribe to colleagues whom they regard as effective teachers; it developed scales for measuring those characteristics which might be useful in quantifying judgments of teaching effectiveness by colleagues; and it explored some relationships between these scales and other variables. Five dimensions were given which faculty members use to describe colleagues whom they regard as effective teachers: research activity and recognition, participation in the academic community, intellectual breadth, relations with students, and concern for teaching. Most of the items describe nonclassroom behavior and are only inferentially or indirectly related to classroom behavior. In a study of student descriptions of effective teachers that was conducted at the same time as the colleague study, scales describing a different set of behaviors were obtained: conceptual approach, classroom interaction, presentation clarity, individualism, and dynamism.

WILSON, W. R. "Student Rating Teachers." *Journal of Higher Education*, 1932, *3*, 75–82.

Every undergraduate student appraised each of his classes and each instructor on a rating blank containing thirty-five topics. On reliability, the instructors who had different sections of the same course made a fairly consistent impression upon their various classes. No significant difference was found between ratings given men and women instructors; and no differences were found on basis of academic rank. Large classes were somewhat less satisfactory than were classes of less than forty students.

WINTHROP, H. "Worth of a Colleague." *Improving College and University Teaching,* 1966, *14,* 262–264.

The role of colleague opinion in evaluation of teaching is discussed. The author contends that the majority can label the nonconformist or aggressive teacher as incompetent and convince the administration to take action. Scholarship and publication are often evaluated by peer approval. A reputable scholar may find his work judged to be of poor quality by his colleagues when he is a member of a minority within a department. Much judging of a colleague's worth takes place behind the scenes. Decision-makers in an administrative hierarchy will frequently avoid a confrontation between the faculty members being judged and their judging peers.

WOODBURNE, L. S. "The Qualifications of Superior Faculty Members." *Journal of Higher Education,* 1952, *23,* 377–382.

A case study was made of thirty-two faculty members who had been advanced far more rapidly than were the average. A randomly selected sample of other faculty was used for comparative purposes. A summary of the qualities of both groups as described by the recommending departments showed a clear and distinct combination of qualities for each group. The representative member of the superior group was a brilliant or high-quality research worker, an outstanding or successful teacher possessing imagination, insight, or originality, industry, and integrity. His counterpart was a sound or high-quality research worker, a competent or effective teacher, and a hard worker, possessing thorough knowledge and some originality. There was only a little difference between the groups in the categories of hard work or teaching effectiveness. Of the superior group, 66 percent were characterized as both imaginative or original and hard working, whereas only six percent of their counterparts had both qualities.

WOODRING, P. "Must College Teachers Publish or Perish." *Educational Digest*, 1964, *30*, 35–37.

The prestige of the university rests on the publications of the faculty, declares the author, thus forcing an emphasis on faculty publication performance. Administrative personnel, as well as department chairmen, have little knowledge of their faculty's teaching competencies, and through long tradition they seldom visit classrooms. However, they can read a colleague's publications. A balanced faculty is needed.

YAMAMOTO, K., AND DIZNEY, H. F. "Eight Professors—A Study on College Students' Preferences Among Their Teachers." *Journal of Educational Psychology*, 1966, *57*, 146–150.

The authors studied students' preferences for different types of professors—administrator, socialite, teacher, and researcher—from each of two sources, education and arts and sciences. Three hundred college students responded to a Likert-type inventory of the eight types of college professors. Teacher, researcher, socialite, and administrator were preferred in that order, and education was preferred to arts and sciences as a source.

YONGE, G. D., AND SASSENRATH, J. M. "Student Personality Correlates of Teacher Ratings." *Journal of Educational Psychology*, 1968, *59*, 44–52.

The 227 students taught by three instructors in a course in educational psychology at University of California, Davis, completed an instructor rating form and a personality test. The data consistently revealed that the psychological meaning of the rated factors varies from instructor to instructor—that is, there are significant differences in correlations between the personality and rating scores from instructor to instructor, and different personality characteristics are correlated with a given factor for different instructors. The type of student who tends to rate one instructor high on a given factor may tend to rate another instructor low on the same dimension. The authors conclude that their study does not mean that the ratings were distorted by the personality characteristics of the raters and thus lacked objectivity, and they explain their point of view in detail.

ZOLLITSCH, H. G., AND KAIMANN, R. A. "Should Students Evaluate Faculties?" *Educational Media,* 1970, *2,* 10–12.

A student opinion survey from the Marquette University provided reasonable insights into the professional effectiveness of the academician. The twenty-two-question instrument used has four sections: preparation, presentation, demands upon the student, and personal characteristics. The survey pointed out that there is some need for faculty improvement. Based upon findings of shortcomings, a prescribed program for strengthening those areas could be worked out.

Author Index

239

Subject Index